Praise for
Disciplined Entrepreneurship Startup Tactics

"*Disciplined Entrepreneurship Startup Tactics* is a game-changer for founders. In my career, I have spent significant time working in startups, especially as employee #10 at Jumia, the largest e-commerce company in Africa. When I started the venture development process all over again for a new startup (Bumpa), the Tactics course at MIT helped me stay grounded, providing the right focus and strategy I needed to execute. It gave me the skills and knowledge to thrive as a founder and helped the venture succeed early. This book will help you do the same."

—*Omolara Ajele-Awoyemi, Co-Founder and Operating Partner,* **Fast Forward Venture Studio,** *and Advisor,* **Bumpa**

"This book goes beyond the usual clichés and dives deep into the real-world challenges and opportunities that startups face. The approach within can truly make a difference in your entrepreneurial endeavors. An essential addition to any entrepreneur's toolkit!"

—*Paul English, Co-Founder and CTO,* **Kayak**

"*Disciplined Entrepreneurship Startup Tactics* is an indispensable guide for entrepreneurs looking to build and scale their ventures. This book provides a systematic approach to startup success, from market testing to fundraising and hiring. It's a must-have resource for any founder striving to create lasting impact."

—*Brad Feld, Partner,* **Foundry,** *and Co-Founder,* **Techstars**

"*Disciplined Entrepreneurship Startup Tactics* has revolutionized my approach to entrepreneurship. This book offers practical tactics and actionable advice that have helped my team and me take a more systematic approach to building our business, Memorable AI. Tactics have truly helped us organize our startup around solid foundational principles, test our hypotheses more effectively, and hire the right people. I often refer back to these learnings when discussing with my co-founder and team. Having leveraged the Tactics course at MIT, I can say confidently that following this framework increases the odds of success for any venture. It's a must-read for any founder."

—*Camilo Fosco,* **MIT** *and Founder,* **Memorable AI**

"Having witnessed the journeys of over 3,000 startups as the founder and long-time CEO of MassChallenge, I can confidently say that *Startup Tactics* is an indispensable resource for entrepreneurs building new ventures. Whether you're a first-time founder or a seasoned entrepreneur, this book will help you navigate the complexities of building a successful startup."

—*John Harthorne, Founder,* **MassChallenge,**
and Founder and Managing Director,
Two Lanterns Venture Capital

"From the outside, HubSpot might seem like a smooth up and to the right story. It belies what actually goes on inside. The best way I'd describe HubSpot is two steps forward followed by one step back followed by two steps forward followed by one step back, etc. *Disciplined Entrepreneurship Startup Tactics* provides an experimentation framework helpful for determining what your next two steps forward should be and what to do when you need to take one step back. Startup Tactics is such a valuable continuation of the entrepreneurship lessons we learned at MIT when we were starting HubSpot."

—*Brian Halligan, Co-Founder and Executive Chairman,* **HubSpot**

"As a founder who has experienced the ups and down of starting and scaling a company firsthand, I highly recommend Disciplined Entrepreneurship Startup Tactics. Based on first principles thinking, it shares practical and actionable guidance for founders at every stage and is a valuable resource for anyone striving to build a successful startup."

—*Drew Houston, Co-Founder and CEO,* **Dropbox**

"*Disciplined Entrepreneurship Startup Tactics* offers a fresh perspective on entrepreneurship, emphasizing founder-led skills through a rigorous, systematic approach. I highly recommend it to aspiring entrepreneurs and students who are looking for a framework to develop their strategic and execution skills. From goal setting to hiring, this invaluable book is a comprehensive guide that equips entrepreneurs with the tools they need to succeed."

—*Mo-Yun Lei Fong, Executive Director, STVP, Stanford Engineering Entrepreneurship Center,*
Stanford University

"As a co-founder of Care.com, scaling the organization from start-up stage through five rounds of funding and IPO, I gained a strong appreciation for the entrepreneurial process. *Disciplined Entrepreneurship Startup Tactics* is a resource that will be incredibly helpful to entrepreneurs at any stage. This book provides an action-oriented framework for startup success. Having spent the past 10 years teaching entrepreneurs I know that this book will help founders learn the skills they need to be successful."

—*Donna Levin, CEO, Arthur M. Blank School for Entrepreneurial Leadership,*
Babson College, *and Co-Founder,* **Care.com**

DISCIPLINED ENTREPRENEURSHIP

STARTUP TACTICS

15 TACTICS TO TURN YOUR
BUSINESS PLAN INTO A BUSINESS

DISCIPLINED ENTREPRENEURSHIP

STARTUP TACTICS

PAUL CHEEK

Executive Director
**Martin Trust Center for
MIT Entrepreneurship**

WILEY

Published by John Wiley & Sons, Inc., Hoboken, New Jersey.
Published simultaneously in Canada.

For general information on our other products and services or for technical support, please contact our Customer Care Department within the United States at (800) 762-2974, outside the United States at (317) 572-3993 or fax (317) 572-4002.

Wiley also publishes its books in a variety of electronic formats. Some content that appears in print may not be available in electronic formats. For more information about Wiley products, visit our web site at www.wiley.com.

Library of Congress Cataloging-in-Publication Data is Available:

ISBN 9781394223350 (Cloth)
ISBN 9781394223367 (ePub)
ISBN 9781394223374 (ePDF)

Cover Design and Illustration: Marius Ursache
Author Photo: Brian Tortora

SKY10063301_020924

To my grandfather Donald J Fager, who founded MLMIC Insurance Company to protect both healthcare providers and patients and led it through an acquisition by Berkshire Hathaway. He exemplified living life with a strong raison d'être and remains an inspiration to me.

And, as I've written this book, my wife, Callie, and I welcomed the next generation.
To Kyla, my daughter, our future entrepreneur!

CONTENTS

FOREWORD

I *LOVE* THIS BOOK, and you will too.

This beautifully continues the ethos of the Disciplined Entrepreneurship books and takes it to a new level.

In my books, I presented a systematic view of what to do, why to do it, and when to do it. There was some guidance on how to do it, but not enough. The easy answer is that it could not all be fit into one book. The even more truthful answer is that it took a ton more work to do this. Paul has done that work.

In the MIT way, Paul has not just developed materials but he has tested them with hundreds of entrepreneurs and humbly iterated the materials over and over again to refine them to be more concise and, most of all, to ensure the tactics work. What you have here is the end product of this multiyear process.

What makes this different from other books and so special to me? Let me give you the reasons for my love:

1. **Systematic:** Everything is based in logic and considers the full system.

2. **Comprehensive:** From Foundations to Market Testing to Product Development and finally Resource Acquisition, it touches the bases of what an entrepreneur needs to execute upon.

3. **Actionable:** There is no value unless the knowledge herein can be put into action. It starts with *Tactics,* which takes you down to where the rubber meets the road, and he delivers on this promise.

4. **Accessible:** Not only is this fun to read, but he has broken it all down so it's not overwhelming—you don't feel like you're reading an operator's manual for an aircraft carrier. The illustrations are a wonderful way to summarize key points and make them not just easily understandable but also memorable.

5. **Integrated:** Metcalfe's law states that connectivity creates exponential value. The connections are not only designed into his advice but made explicit.

6. **Proven:** As mentioned previously, this material has been tested in many different environments as you see by the examples, and refined. You are not getting version 1.0.

In summary, it is an engineering approach to entrepreneurship that has been desperately needed. Yes, entrepreneurship is a mindset, but that mindset is not effective unless it is coupled with the necessary execution skills. Those skills come about by getting good guidance, which is what this book provides in spades.

To say I am excited to see the book coming out is an understatement. Never have entrepreneurs been more important to society and our future. We need more and better ones who are connected by a common language so they can continue to develop. Fortunately, now with this book, they have never had better materials to support them in excelling in this craft going forward. Read on—you will never regret it.

—Bill Aulet
Author of Disciplined Entrepreneurship;
Ethernet Inventors Professor of the Practice
of Entrepreneurship, MIT Sloan School of Management;
and Managing Director, Martin Trust Center for MIT Entrepreneurship

ACKNOWLEDGMENTS

I MUST START BY thanking my students. This book would not be possible without them—or it wouldn't be nearly as good. I have had the opportunity to work with thousands of students both here at MIT and around the world. My work with them has led to the revisions that make this book so rigorous. Not only have my students helped me to refine the contents within but they make my job so rewarding.

I am also deeply indebted to Bill Aulet, who has opened up many of the opportunities that have led me to publish this book. His work in Disciplined Entrepreneurship is the foundation for *Startup Tactics*. I remember the first time we discussed *Tactics* and since then he has pushed me to develop more and more content to help us work towards our mission at the Trust Center of advancing the field of innovation-driven entrepreneurship.

Speaking of the Trust Center, our leadership at MIT, including the chair of MIT Corporation, MIT's board of trustees, Mark Gorenberg, and our president, Sally Kornbluth, have demonstrated their commitment to entrepreneurship and their support of our work at the Trust Center, which serves as a significant source of motivation to continue pushing the boundaries of entrepreneurship education. And our leadership at MIT Sloan—including Dave Schmittlein, Michael Cusumano, Nelson Repenning, Scott Stern, our founder Ed Roberts, and partners in the MIT School of Engineering led by Anantha Chandrakasan—have been incredibly supportive of my work and the development of the course upon which this book is based. The course, Venture Creation Tactics, is one that I am fortunate to lead alongside my co-instructors, Nagarjuna Venna and George Whitfield, who have been incredibly influential in the development of what we now refer to as "Startup Tactics." None of this would be possible without our *amazing* team at the Trust Center past and present. Many thanks to my colleagues Andy Acevedo, Neelesh Bagga, Mac Cameron, Alicia Carelli, Carly Chase, Elaine Chen, Trish Cotter, Kit Hickey, Alfredo Garcia, Christine Hsieh, Mona Jones, Macauley Kenney, Amrutha Killada, Jenny Larios Berlin, Kosta Ligris, Tommy Long, Leah Lovgren, Ylana Lopez, Stephanie MacConnell, Erin Martin, Nick Meyer, Susan Neal, Magali Paoli, Will Sanchez, Devon Sherman Daley, Navroop Singh Sehmi, Ben Soltoff, Doug Williams, and Greg Wymer. Special appreciation for Dip Patel, former Trust Center Entrepreneur in Residence, for his inspiration and contributions to the Tactics framework. I also wish to thank our entire teaching faculty at the Trust Center who lead the variety of courses in our portfolio.

Our many collaborators at MIT have helped me to move the development of Startup Tactics and other related entrepreneurship initiatives forward, including Jinane Abounadi, Marty Culpepper, Oli de Weck, Benoit Forget, Sherwin Greenblatt, Marissa Gross, Jeffrey Grossman, Paula Hammond, John Hart, Dan Hastings, Peter Hirst, Travis Hunter, Ali Jadbabaie, Ann Marie Maxwell, Lesley Millar-Nicholson, Murat Onen, Alisia Pajevic, Asu Ozdaglar, Jacquelyn Pless, Bob Pozen, Reza Rahaman, Leon Sandler, Joel Schindall, Don Shobrys, Zoltán Spakovszky, Akshit Singla, Alula Sherifew, Alfred Spector, Anne White, and Rob Whiting.

And of course our wonderful collaborators at other institutions. Rowena Barrett, Glen Murphy, Graham Fellows, Peta Ellis, and the rest of the QUT Entrepreneurship team at the Queensland University of Technology in Brisbane, Australia, who ran a concurrent Tactics course with their students. Daniela Ruiz Massieu, of ITAM, who joined our Tactics course at MIT during her sabbatical and has provided invaluable input into the content development. Jeff Larsen and the Dal Innovates team at Dalhousie University for enabling me to experiment with the Tactics content in several of their programs. And Charlie Tillett, who has kindly shared his financial model template with our students and readers of this book.

Much of what I have learned about entrepreneurship stems earlier in my professional career and has been enabled by my family, who have provided tremendous support—especially my wife, Callie. Much of this book is based on my learnings through my entrepreneurial journey founding and building new ventures alongside Calum Barnes, Vikram Chabra, Vanessa Coleman, Braden Golub, Bay Hudner, Rob Ianelli, Monil Kothari, C. Todd Lombardo, Sacha Nacar, Joe Nigro, and Patrick Todd. I regularly use examples from our experiences together to help my students and without you these experiences wouldn't exist!

You would not be reading this book without those who believed in it before it existed. Specifically, the lead illustrator Marius Ursache, who somehow always knows *exactly* how to communicate the key points in fun cartoons, contributors Matt Volpi, Kelly Talbot, Anastasia Lysenko, and publishers Shannon Vargo, Deborah Schindlar, Leah Zarra, and Gabby Mancuso of John Wiley & Sons. They all believed in this book from the beginning and helped to bring it to publication.

Thank you all!

INTRODUCTION TO TACTICS

Our society is creating more problems in the world around us than solutions. This fundamental challenge is best addressed by entrepreneurs driven by passion, vision, and opportunity. Entrepreneurs, of course, aren't just startup founders. Entrepreneurs are also found in corporations, academic institutions, government, nonprofits, NGOs, and elsewhere as both founders and employees. Entrepreneurs are vital to our society's forward progress, but they must maximize their limited time and money, and stay scrappy. This book will help you, as a current or future entrepreneur, do precisely that.

In this book, I'll share tactics based on my experience as a successful entrepreneur, insights I've gained from other entrepreneurs, and through my experiences as an entrepreneurship educator at the Massachusetts Institute of Technology. These are tactics I've used when building my businesses and that I've found most effective from my work with thousands of startup founders around the world. I'll teach you these skills and demonstrate how to use them through a systematic approach. These entrepreneurial skills will enable you to make a greater impact in the world as a startup founder or in your organization by creating *new* things using the existing resources already on hand. Won't your boss be excited to hear that?

The proof points and learnings you gather from early go-to-market tactics will help you sell to additional stakeholders—whether that's a new engineer you want to bring on board or an investor you'd like to raise money from. These potential stakeholders have many opportunities to choose from, so you must develop and present evidence to prove that your opportunity is the most compelling.

While certain specifics might not directly apply to every industry, these tactics are meant for any entrepreneur and are particularly of use during the early stages of any venture. This mindset and approach will help you evaluate and hone your early go-to-market approach. Even engineers and product developers will come away with a completely new view of taking a nascent concept to market.

You will find examples within that are simple and can be easily digested, but this book is not a one-size-fits-all approach. It is up to you to take what you learn from this book and apply it in the development of your business.

Because you already have your own specific expertise, I will share with you three promises that we make to participants from around the world in our Entrepreneurship Development Program at the Trust Center. As you read this book:

1. You will learn something you already know.

2. You will learn something you didn't know.

3. You will get as much out of this book as you put into it.

With that in mind, know that this book is designed to expand your entrepreneurial mindset, skillset, and mode of operating for everything you do.

Next Frontier of Entrepreneurship Education

During my years working in the Martin Trust Center for MIT Entrepreneurship, I have taught more than 5,000 students and advised more than 500 startups. Some students I work with weekly for years, while others I've met with just once in their journeys.

Of course, this represents a tiny fraction of the entrepreneurs around the world working on solving big problems. They, too, can benefit from the content we teach at MIT, so I've taken as much material as possible that I cover during office hours, workshops, and classes and included it in this book.

When I first began working with student entrepreneurs at MIT, I found myself constantly revisiting the same topics during one-on-one office hours. These conversations typically boiled down to students asking for help on how to build a product, raise money for their startup, and recruit early technical talent, including technical co-founders. More often than not, I encouraged these entrepreneurs to pump the brakes and instead focus first on getting traction with customers. This isn't just a delay tactic, but rather a necessary and prudent change to the order of operations.

No one wants to invest their money or bet their career on a product without confidence in its potential and some facts and data to support that assumption. And, contrary to what many first-time founders may think, you don't need a pile of cash or a hot-shot CTO to test out some hypotheses and get a sense of whether you're on the right path to finding product-market fit.

The reality is that startups need meaningful traction to justify moving forward with hiring and fundraising. Sales represent that traction, but you also need something to sell, which means you, the founder, must wear a lot of hats. That requires training in a variety of skills and functional areas. You can learn these skills and go to market before hiring anyone or productizing anything.

These topics were so popular among students that I began offering workshops. The demand for these proved so great that I then turned them into a full course on venture creation tactics, which is the foundation of the book you're now reading.

My work at the Trust Center, which manifests in this book, is based on lived experience out in industry as an entrepreneur. I recount my experiences co-founding three companies and advising countless others. Now I have the opportunity to share these experiences with you. I reveal details of how we systematically built these businesses. There is no magic power that I or anybody else has. I simply followed the process of applying these tactics.

Context of Theory, Practice, and Tactics

Entrepreneurship has traditionally been taught through theory and practice. Theory is the strategy with a long time horizon, which doesn't change frequently. Practice covers the frameworks and concepts representing first principles and fundamentals. Both are necessary for any and every entrepreneur.

But entrepreneurs who have learned the theory and practice have been left hanging. Far too often they don't have the opportunity to learn steps for taking a systematic, structured approach to learning the tactics of entrepreneurship. Tactics help entrepreneurs acquire the necessary skills to turn their business plan into an actual business.

The integration of theory, practice, and tactics is what leads to highly effective venture development. Entrepreneurs increase their odds of success when their tactics are tied directly to their strategy. Should you ever find yourself on historic Market Street in downtown Charleston, South Carolina, in the US, pop into Church and Union restaurant. Inside your eyes will adjust to the dim light of the old church building and be drawn to the ceiling. Look up and see if you can find this quote:

Strategy without tactics is the slowest route to victory. Tactics without strategy is the noise before defeat.

A local artist hand-wrote this on the ceiling of the restaurant in 2021, but these words actually date back 2,500 years to when Chinese military strategist Sun Tzu wrote *The Art of War,* and in fact the whole text is painted across the ceiling. Tzu makes this point to emphasize that you must have both strategy and tactics together. In the context of entrepreneurship, strategy is your business plan and tactics are more concrete steps and actions taken to get you where you need to go.

Rooted in First Principles

Anyone can build a business by learning and applying the tactics presented in this book. While these tactics can help you get started, it's important to recognize they're all designed to be rooted in the first principles of entrepreneurship. These are business fundamentals that—if overlooked—lead to a less efficient, less valuable business. After spending years studying entrepreneurship fundamentals, I can confidently say that a thorough understanding of them is required to execute these tactics with excellence.

Each tactic is related to the entrepreneurship fundamentals described in *Disciplined Entrepreneurship,* the book authored by fellow MIT faculty member, co-instructor, and friend Bill Aulet. If you haven't already familiarized yourself with *Disciplined Entrepreneurship,* you will surely find the methodology helpful. *Disciplined Entrepreneurship* presents 24 steps to a successful startup. These steps start by addressing the question "Who is our customer?" and proceed with the various components required for a strong business plan.

SIX THEMES:

I WHO IS YOUR CUSTOMER?	II WHAT CAN YOU DO FOR YOUR CUSTOMER?	III HOW DOES YOUR CUSTOMER ACQUIRE YOUR PRODUCT?	IV HOW DO YOU MAKE MONEY OFF YOUR PRODUCT?	V HOW DO YOU DESIGN AND BUILD YOUR PRODUCT?	VI HOW DO YOU SCALE YOUR BUSINESS?
1 MARKET SEGMENTATION — **WHAT?** Brainstorm and identify how your idea/technology can serve a variety of potential end users. Primary market research (PMR) is then used to fill out a matrix. **WHY?** It is crucial to start the process with the customer and work everything back from there.	**5 BEACHHEAD MARKET PERSONA** — **WHAT?** Identify one actual real end user in your Beachhead Market that best represents your End User Profile. **WHY?** Creates great focus in your organization and serves as a touchstone for all decisions going forward.	**9 FIRST 10 CUSTOMERS** — **WHAT?** Create a list of the next 10 customers after the Persona who closely fit the end user profile. **WHY?** Validates the Persona and all the assumptions you have made so far.	**13 CUSTOMER ACQUISITION PROCESS** — **WHAT?** Detail how the DMU decides to buy your product. Particular focus will be made to identify Windows of Opportunity and Triggers (Step 13A) where they are most open to acquiring. **WHY?** This will be critical input to determine the length of the sales cycle and identify critical bottlenecks in the process.	**17 CUSTOMER LIFETIME VALUE (LTV)** — **WHAT?** Estimate the Net Present Value (NPV) of the total profits you will get from a new customer over the time period they will be your customer. **WHY?** To complete the unit economics, you now need to estimate and understand the drivers of the LTV and it should get to at least 3X the CoCA.	**21 KEY ASSUMPTIONS TESTING** — **WHAT?** Test, through a series of small and inexpensive experiments, each of the individual assumptions you have identified in Step 20. **WHY?** This scientific approach will allow you to understand which assumptions are valid or not, then adjust when the cost of doing so is lower.
2 BEACHHEAD MARKET — **WHAT?** Select one market segment from Step 1 where you feel you have the highest odds of success while also giving you legitimacy and strategic assets to grow further. **WHY?** As a startup you have limited resources and focus is essential.	**6 FULL LIFE CYCLE USE CASE** — **WHAT?** Describe the full longitudinal experience of the persona and what opportunity there is for improvement. **WHY?** This will provide invaluable information for future steps to create specificity with regard to solutions, value and accessing the customer.	**10 CORE & MOATS** — **WHAT?** Determine the single thing that you will do better than anyone else that will be very difficult for others to copy. **WHY?** Having a clear definition of your Core will allow you to focus your limited resources to build and reinforce it.	**14 TOTAL ADDRESSABLE MARKET (TAM) SIZE FOR FOLLOW-ON MARKETS** — **WHAT?** Calculate the annual revenues from the top follow-on markets after you are successful in your Beachhead Market. **WHY?** It shows the potential that can come from winning your beachhead and motivates you to do so quickly and effectively.	**18 SCALABLE REVENUE ENGINE** — **WHAT?** Visually map the short-, medium- and long-term way you will create and fulfill demand for your product. **WHY?** This will be critical input to calculating the CoCA over time.	**22 MINIMUM VIABLE BUSINESS PRODUCT (MVBP)** — **WHAT?** Define a minimal product to start the customer feedback loop—where the customer gets value from the product and pays for it. **WHY?** Reduce the variables in the equation to get customer feedback successfully while simultaneously being resource-efficient.
3 END-USER PROFILE — **WHAT?** Use PMR techniques to build out a robust demographic and psychographic description of your end user. **WHY?** There are 3 reasons: (1) to keep the focus on the end user, (2) to deepen your understanding of the primary customer, and (3) to calculate the TAM in the next step.	**7 HIGH-LEVEL PRODUCT SPECIFICATION** — **WHAT?** Create a visual description of the product as well as making a simple draft brochure, landing page, or digital representation of the proposed product. **WHY?** You need to make sure your team and the customer all have a common agreement on what the product is.	**11 CHART YOUR COMPETITIVE POSITION** — **WHAT?** Represent visually your position relative to the other alternatives in the Persona's top two priorities. **WHY?** Customers don't care about your "core" but they do care about benefits relating to their priorities.	**15 BUSINESS MODEL** — **WHAT?** Review the different types of way to get paid for your product and chose the best one aligned with all key stakeholders' interests. **WHY?** Wise selection of a value extraction Business Model can dramatically reduce CoCA, increase Lifetime Value (LTV) of an Acquired Customer and provide you with competitive advantage.	**19 COST OF CUSTOMER ACQUISITION (COCA)** — **WHAT?** Estimate the total marketing and sales expense in a given period to get new customers and divide this by the number of new customers. **WHY?** The unit economics are a simple but effective proxy for how sustainable and attractive your business will be at scales.	**23 PROOF THAT DOGS WILL EAT THE DOG FOOD** — **WHAT?** Offer your MVBP to your target customer and obtain quantitative metrics regarding the adoption rate, the value the target customer is getting, and proof that someone is paying for it. **WHY?** Numbers don't lie. Show concrete evidence, not simply anecdotal evidence.
4 BEACHHEAD TOTAL ADDRESSABLE MARKET (TAM) SIZE — **WHAT?** Estimate the revenue per year you will get in your Beachhead Market if you achieve 100% market share. **WHY?** To make sure your Beachhead Market is not too big or too small.	**8 QUANTIFIED VALUE PROPOSITION** — **WHAT?** Summarize in as concrete a way as possible the value your product will create for the target customer. **WHY?** Customers buy based on value; it needs to be clear that you can show it.	**12 CUSTOMER'S DECISION-MAKING UNIT (DMU)** — **WHAT?** Determine all the people who are involved in making the decision to acquire your product, including influencers. **WHY?** This starts the process to determine the Cost of Customer Acquisition (CoCA).	**16 PRICING FRAMEWORK** — **WHAT?** Determine a framework to test pricing for your new product and decide on what the initial price will be. **WHY?** Small changes in pricing can have a huge impact on your profitability.	**20 KEY ASSUMPTIONS IDENTIFICATION** — **WHAT?** Identify key assumptions to be tested before you begin to make heavy investments in product development. **WHY?** It will be faster and much less costly now to test the assumptions and allow you to preserve valuable resources and adjust as needed.	**24 PRODUCT PLAN** — **WHAT?** Develop a longer-term plan to add functionality so you can address additional markets over time. **WHY?** It is important to think ahead and have a plan so your team is ready to keep moving forward after the MVBP.

The 24 Steps are incredibly helpful for building a business plan and they can be expanded upon with tactics to gather larger-scale evidence that a business opportunity is real and empower you with the related skills necessary to turn your plan into action. Regardless of whether you built your business plan using the 24 Steps, you will find that these tactics can be used to verify your work thus far.

If you did leverage the 24 Steps, you can take the plan developed and begin to execute. Not every step maps one-to-one with a tactic. There is a one-to-many relationship. Each tactic relates to multiple steps from the 24 Steps. We'll walk through these tactics so that you can confirm your findings and get a paying customer. For example, putting these tactics into practice will enable you to further validate your Persona from Step 5, ensure your customer Lifetime Value (LTV) from Step 17 is actually greater than your CoCA from Step 19, sign up your Next 10 Customers beyond those from Step 9, and more. Data-backed, and all without a full "product."

Throughout this book you will find helpful reminders of relevant steps from *Disciplined Entrepreneurship* to help you as you relate the tactics back to the first principles of entrepreneurship.

Investing in Individuals, Not Startups

Our data at the Martin Trust Center for MIT Entrepreneurship supports the educational approach to teaching individuals rather than simply helping them start companies. Throughout this book you will learn the entrepreneurial skills needed to start new ventures and increase your odds of success.

Research conducted by Professor Daniela Ruiz Massieu, Managing Director of the Instituto Tecnologico Autonomo de Mexico (ITAM) Entrepreneurship and Innovation Center, and her collaborator from ITAM, Professor Claudia Gonzalez-Brambila, demonstrates the impact this approach has on entrepreneurs.[1] They analyzed the first ten years of startups that came through MIT's startup accelerator at the Trust Center, MIT delta v.

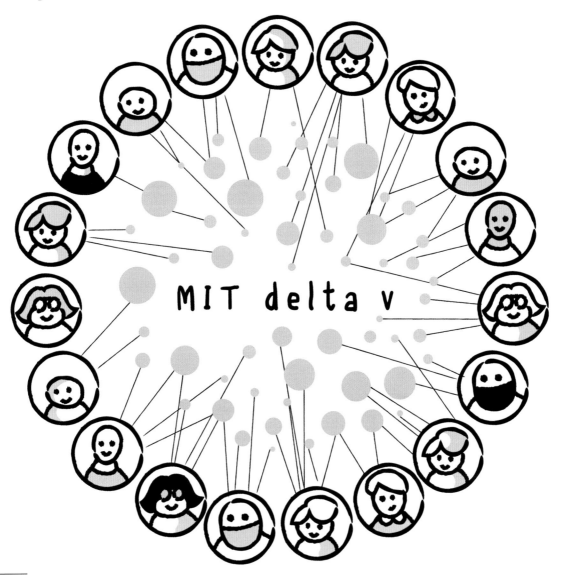

---

[1] https://entrepreneurship.mit.edu/delta-v-10-year-study/

We were incredibly excited to learn from their report that those 181 startups have raised $1 billion and 61% are either still operating or were acquired. While a number of factors play into a startup's long-term viability and companies founded by MIT students have a number of innate advantages, this rate significantly outpaces the industry average and is a testament to our model's real-world success.

Due to our investment in the long-term entrepreneurial success of these individuals, we're even more pleased to see what they've done with those learnings beyond those delta v startups. This same cohort of entrepreneurs have founded an additional 130 companies after delta v, which have raised not $1 billion, but $2 billion.

One of my goals when developing these tactics was increasing the number of qualified applicants to our delta v accelerator by equipping founders with tools to test out their hypotheses and find traction before applying to and joining the program. We're seeing results already, as the tactics help bridge business plan theories to real traction for more and more of the young businesses applying to delta v in the past few years.

One such example is Livvi, co-founded by Madeleine Cooney and Anisha Quadir. Using the tactics in this book, they secured a 1,500-plus waitlist of potential customers before applying to delta v. This impressive traction increased our confidence in their plan and we welcomed them to the program, where they could follow their vision with greater conviction thanks to these early signals of product-market fit.

The tactics in this book may not always directly relate to the specific challenges you're currently facing as you launch your venture and once you reach scale, and they may be less applicable in some cases. But they form a solid foundation for executing any startup vision or even a new product launch and may come in handy down the line with your current business or during another future entrepreneurial adventure, supporting you in your long-term development as an entrepreneur.

Founder-Led Everything: Wearing Many Hats

As entrepreneurs at MIT, we begin by doing what all good engineers do: we define our terms. So what exactly is a tactic?

> ***tactic (noun)***
> *an action carefully planned to achieve a specific end*

Founders must execute a variety of actions to build a successful business. Entrepreneurs with professional experience in one functional area often specialize there, and it is important for entrepreneurs to have a specialty. Mine, for example, is engineering. But it is my familiarity with business fundamentals and with each functional area that makes me so effective in the early stages of launching new ventures.

Because entrepreneurs deal with the entirety of the business during its critical early stages, they need to feel just as comfortable whiteboarding data flows as they are cold-calling prospects and giving an elevator pitch to a venture capitalist. No one brings all those skills to the table, but these tactics create the scaffolding for the versatile leader you will become.

For example, one topic entrepreneurs raise often is "founder-led sales," which is grounded in the notion that the organization's founder is always selling what the organization has to offer.

This remains true often until the organization has scaled to hundreds of employees. Even then, the largest deals are often still closed by the founder.

While founder-led sales is a critical component for new ventures, I would argue that it's founder-led *everything* that makes the difference. Before adding dedicated resources, the founder is responsible for executing in each functional area, which means founders need the skills to drive every aspect of their new business forward. As resources are added, it becomes the founder's responsibility not to execute or apply the tactic themselves, but instead to effectively communicate with those responsible for the tactic.

Each tactic will provide you with the experience to execute and communicate effectively:

Stage	#	Name	Role Training
Intro	0	Intro	Entrepreneur!
Foundations	1	Goals	COO
	2	Systems	Head of IT
Market Testing	3	Market Research	Founder
	4	Assets	Graphic Designer
	5	Marketing	CMO
	6	Sales	CRO / VP of Sales
Product Development	7	Product Roadmap	Product Manager
	8	Design	Designer
	9	User Testing	User Researcher
	10	Engineering	VP of Engineering
Resource Acquisition	11	Legal	General Counsel
	12	Finance	CFO
	13	Pitch Deck Design	CMO
	14	Fundraising	CEO
	15	Hiring	Chief People Officer

These tactics enable entrepreneurs to improve their odds of success in the early days of building a new venture, which enables them to solve our world's biggest challenges. These tactics help founders in the earliest stages of launching a new venture execute in each of the functional areas necessary to get the traction needed to acquire resources to scale the business. Ultimately these newfound resources will enable founders to transition their role from that of a generalist to that of a specialist: an entrepreneurial leader.

It's Never Too Late to Leverage These Tactics

These tactics will prepare you to be scrappy whether you're just starting your first company, you already have traction, you're building your third company, or something else. We always need to be scrappy, even after raising a pile of cash or landing major customers. I recall a conversation with Hisham Anwar, the co-founder of BrightBytes. Before the company's acquisition by Google, Hisham and his team had raised over $50M in funding. Anwar told me that if he knew in advance all the things he eventually learned through the entrepreneurial process about how to maximize his resources he could probably have achieved the same outcome with just $5M. That doesn't just mean he could do it cheaper, but that he'd also have retained significantly more equity while reaching key milestones even faster.

But you're not behind if you've already started building. These tactics can help regardless of how far along you are in your current venture or haven't begun one at all.

One concrete example is Camilo Fosco, a PhD candidate at MIT in the Computer Science and Artificial Intelligence Laboratory (CSAIL). He joined my Venture Creation Tactics course at MIT to learn the entrepreneurship tactics needed to take his company, Memorable AI, to the next level. Memorable AI's team had already surpassed 20 people and they'd raised $3M+ before he enrolled in the class.

Memorable AI is an artificial intelligence company developing deep learning models to predict the impact of videos and image-based advertisements. Their software predicts the response that proposed advertisements will have, recommends improvements to increase effectiveness, and designs new potential advertisements.

Despite having a solid foundation for his business, Fosco leveraged the tactics he learned to further improve his business. First, he developed new and more effective startup assets, including a completely redesigned brand and animations that communicate their complex value proposition in a matter of seconds. Second, he was able to refine the company's sales process. He had a sales pipeline already and used the tactics to fine-tune, experiment, and systematize the process, which led to Memorable AI signing and onboarding four large, brand-name clients. Third, Fosco and his team improved their culture and recruiting with intentionality.

The company identified high-value talent pipelines and actually recruited candidates for their next hires, which allowed the business to redesign and optimize its organizational chart.

Fosco and his team leveraged these tactics to maximize their runway using the limited time and funds Memorable AI had already raised. This illustrates the fact that it is never too late to learn these tactics and apply them to become a more resourceful and disciplined entrepreneur.

Field Manual No. 22-100

While it's never too late to employ these tactics, it will always remain your job to understand them. This remains true as you transition from wearing every hat as entrepreneur extraordinaire in the early stages of your venture into an entrepreneurial leader. Leadership is one of the many qualities of individuals that is developed by the military. In Field Manual No. 22-100, titled Military Leadership, published in 1990 by the Department of the Army, Carl E. Vuono, then general and chief of staff in the United States Army, proclaims that leaders must learn to "fulfill the expectations of all soldiers" and lists the demonstration of tactical competence as the first of these expectations:

> *Demonstrate tactical and technical competence.*
> *Know your business. Soldiers expect their leaders to be tactically and technically competent. Soldiers want to follow those leaders who are confident of their own abilities. To be confident a leader must first be competent. Trust between soldiers and their leaders is based on the secure knowledge that the leader is competent.*[2]

Vuono continues on that it becomes the leader's job to teach others and to stress the basic fundamentals. In your entrepreneurial journey you will find that it becomes very easy, and instinctual, to veer off from the basic fundamentals of the entrepreneurial pursuit. Much like a military leader, you as an entrepreneur are on a mission and you and your team will be tackling difficult tasks in situations where success is less than likely. As Vuono explains, "To achieve excellence in these tasks, leaders must explain the importance of the mission, articulate priorities, and focus soldier and unit efforts to perform in an efficient and disciplined manner. Well led, properly trained, motivated, and inspired soldiers will accomplish any mission."

You and your team can achieve your entrepreneurial mission. To do so you must understand the tactics, and you must practice them, routinely returning to the references you have on hand in this book, which will enable you to maintain focus on the mission in front of you.

---

[2] https://armyoe.files.wordpress.com/2018/03/1990-fm-22-100.pdf

Experimentation Mindset: Get Your Lab Coat

Your mission is important, but it can't be achieved with predefined approaches alone. These tactics require structured creativity, or calculated experimentation. We can take inspiration from Franklin Delano Roosevelt's 1932 speech on the need for experimentation and its critical role in the development of a better world around us:

> *The country needs and, unless I mistake its temper, the country demands bold, persistent experimentation. It is common sense to take a method and try it: If it fails, admit it frankly and try another. But above all, try something.*

For those with a founder-led everything mindset, we need to recognize that not everything will work as expected. And, instead of bemoaning the lack of certainty, we should embrace the learnings and opportunities these unforeseen detours and obstacles provide.

Scientists embrace this approach, carefully and diligently trying one tweak after another, measuring the results of each test before plotting their next step, and using the scientific method to explore the unknown. As an entrepreneur, you have a *lot* of unknowns, but you can also employ the scientific method to deal with them. It begins with observation, forming hypotheses, and developing controlled experiments to collect and analyze data. This data informs the next steps forward.

Compared to large organizations with extensive historical data that can be mined and incorporated into the decision-making process, you're likely making decisions with limited data. This disadvantage can be mitigated by using an experimental method approach to each of the tactics. Every experiment will add to your knowledge base, helping you make the most informed decisions possible. In turn, this reduces risk and increases the odds of success for a new venture.

Executing each tactic launches another search for a signal in the noise. You're looking for another proof point that de-risks the business you're building. Regardless of whether you're a scientist, a marketing whiz, or a sales superstar, grab your lab coat and prepare to use each tactic to run experiments.

Tactical Stages

Tactics are integrated and iterative, designed to be learned in a specific order but executed in harmony. These tactics give you the knowledge, know-how, and confidence to execute important tasks critical for your venture that might be a little outside your comfort zone and areas of expertise.

The tactics and supporting educational content are not designed to make every entrepreneur the most skilled recruiter, for example, with every trick known to professional recruiters. As my co-instructor Nagarjuna Venna says, these tactics are designed to help founders learn just enough about each role to apply them for a short period of time effectively. They're especially valuable during the early days of a new venture when the founder is responsible for every functional area. However, even after your business finds its footing and grows into a larger and more sophisticated company, you'll still tap these foundational learnings on a regular basis to manage different business function leaders, provide guidance and leadership to employees, and to make important strategic decisions at the executive level.

To mirror the evolution of a new venture, the tactics are divided up into four different stages throughout this book: foundations, market testing, product development, and resource acquisition. When I refer to resource acquisition in this book I mean securing additional resources to fuel your venture. More specifically, this includes fundraising, securing more money, and hiring, securing more time. As you apply the tactics within, you and your business will graduate from one stage to the next, traversing from initial ideation to scaling up the team.

As we explore each tactic in this book you can expect an introduction to the tactic, a specific approach to applying the tactic, tools of the trade including software and services recommendations to accelerate applying the tactic, prompts of what you can do next to apply the tactic, and references to the *Startup Tactics Workbook* series. Every tactic has an accompanying workbook that you can use as you apply what you learn in this book. Most tactics will include examples of how others have implemented the tactic.

Many of the examples included are from students in two of the courses I teach—15.390 New Enterprises and 15.388 Venture Creation Tactics—while in their degree programs who have generously allowed me to share their work with you. These examples are not always complete because of time limitations in our courses, but always illustrate best practices that represent the real-world entrepreneurial process. The projects described within may not always have turned into full-fledged companies depending on the decisions that each entrepreneur made after completing their coursework, but the examples illustrate their educational milestones and will surely help you.

Throughout the book, I'll use many organizations, vendors, and banks as examples. This is done to illustrate the concepts being discussed and isn't intended to be an endorsement for or against any particular organization. You should evaluate organizations and vendors referenced and make the most informed decision for you and your business.

To give you a preview of what's to come, let's introduce you to each stage.

Stage 1: Foundations

Building a business with strong goals and systems is a lot like building a physical structure. You need a sound foundation constructed to support everything eventually built atop it.

This doesn't mean you need to rent a giant office before you've hired your first employee or buy a Super Bowl ad to reach your first customer. It means using tactics to intentionally define the values, mission, vision, and early measures of success. These bedrock principles will guide everyone's actions and ensure your limited resources and energy get channeled into the activities and initiatives that matter most. Establishing these core goals and continually referencing and revising them keeps everyone's eyes on the same prize.

This stage also includes the identification, selection, and adoption of core systems the organization needs to effectively manage activities and facilitate the tactics in subsequent stages.

Tactic 1: Goals

WHAT? Turning your vision into shorter-term goals and those goals into to-dos.

WHY? The process of defining strong goals and sticking to them seems simple until the rubber meets the road.

Tactic 2: Systems

WHAT? Identifying the most flexible tools and systems to manage the business and track progress towards KPIs.

WHY? The team needs to be aligned on the systems to use and those systems might not be the ones that are used in large organizations.

Stage 2: Market Testing

Not every idea is a winner, so it's important to test our assumptions and hypotheses as quickly and cheaply as possible. You want to be sure you're onto something that really resonates with your target market before committing resources and heavily investing in it, no matter how much experience you have as an entrepreneur or how much confidence you and your team have about something. No one picks a winner every time, so the sooner you know whether you're heading in the right or wrong direction the better.

Leveraging our foundational goals keeps us on track and we can lean on our systems as we move forward with market testing to both validate that real people want our proposed product and build out our early go-to-market approach. These activities include primary market research, visual asset creation, and demand generation through marketing and sales.

Tactic 3: Market Research

WHAT? Unlocking unique insights from market research including both primary and secondary, starting with qualitative and shifting to quantitative.

WHY? Quantifying qualitative research helps to communicate the unique insights gained from the process.

Tactic 4: Assets

WHAT? Building visuals to share with potential customers that describe the value created through a website, graphics, animations, and videos.

WHY? You're offering something new to the world and have limited time to communicate its value. Visuals help!

Tactic 5: Marketing

WHAT? Running marketing campaigns targeted specifically at your end users to evaluate demand and refine value propositions.

WHY? You need a waitlist or preorders to justify investing in product development. You need to attract exclusively your end users.

Tactic 6: Sales

WHAT? Building lead lists and outbound messaging targeted at your end users.

WHY? Marketing will fill your top of funnel, but outbound outreach will help you to sign on customers, especially if building a B2B business.

Stage 3: Product Development

Assuming market testing confirms that your idea is getting traction with prospects, you'll have a waiting list of customers anxious to try out your product. So now you've got to build it. This can be tedious and boring for visionaries or the best stage of the whole thing for the geekier founders, but regardless, it's another critical juncture in your venture's evolution.

Of course, product development isn't just mindless execution. It encompasses product roadmapping, design, user testing, and engineering, not to mention building out all the supporting functions and operations to launch, sell, deliver, and support the products you're offering.

Tactic 7: Product Roadmap

WHAT? Mapping your product vision down to a product strategy so that you focus on building the right things.

WHY? You can easily start building every feature under the sun, but tying product development activities back to organization level goals and your product vision will conserve resources.

Tactic 8: Design

WHAT? Designing your product starting with something as simple as a sketch and slowly increasing fidelity.

WHY? Design is much faster and cheaper to change than fully built products. Starting with design allows you to make rapid tweaks before beginning engineering.

Tactic 9: User Testing

WHAT? Before beginning the development of a product you can test directly with users to get feedback, much like we do in conducting primary market research.

WHY? Rapid iterations with user testing feedback on designs helps to refine the product before diving deep into engineering.

Tactic 10: Engineering

WHAT? Identifying the lowest-tech path to building the minimum viable business product.

WHY? You might be able to build your product yourself and rapidly iterate before hiring technical talent or outsourcing to conserve resources.

Stage 4: Resource Acquisition

With the market validated, customers in the queue, and a product developed, it's time to move onto resource acquisition. While you likely didn't get to a full product release all by yourself, once you've shipped your first orders and confirmed product-market fit, it's much easier to add both senior staff and junior headcount.

You'll have money coming in, which can offset some of those additional salaries, and you can offer less total equity thanks to the business's higher valuations. Your venture also becomes more attractive to a wider pool of applicants because they know they're joining a real business with shipping products and actual customers.

The resource acquisition stage includes incorporation, finance, and pitch deck design before fundraising and hiring.

Tactic 11: Legal

WHAT? Finding legal representation, incorporating your business, and getting familiar with the legalese that you will certainly run into.

WHY? You will need to incorporate and should find the right time to do so. Legal representation can be expensive so you want to be as best educated as possible.

Tactic 12: Finance

WHAT? Building a robust financial model based on what you've learned in previous tactics to demonstrate a path to profitability.

WHY? You need a financial model to communicate the opportunity you have for both investors and potential new recruits.

Tactic 13: Pitch Deck

WHAT? Designing a compelling pitch deck about your business and traction to date.

WHY? You need more than a deck; you need a story. A story will engage others and your slides can be built to support it.

Tactic 14: Fundraising

WHAT? Evaluate the potential sources of funding, identify potential investors, develop your fundraising assets, and then run the fundraising process.

WHY? You don't have time to speak to every investor. Instead you need to focus your efforts on the best fit funders for you and your business.

Tactic 15: Hiring

WHAT? Identify gaps in your team's skills, build a job description, source candidates, and recruit them onto your team.

WHY? Hiring is how you open up additional bandwidth with more time on your team. An intentional approach will help you land the top talent.

How to Use This Book

This book is intended to help you learn each of the tactics right now—while reading. It is also designed to be a reference while you develop your venture.

As you develop your venture, once you have started with a tactic, you should never stop applying it as you continue to develop the business, but there generally is no sense in applying a subsequent tactic for the first time until you have applied the tactic prior.

As you read this book, you will not always need the tactic in the moment, but practicing the execution of the tactic in the order described here will help you to prepare for when you need it most. That might be in building your current venture, or it might be useful to you in the future. Consequently, it would be ideal to read this book in sequential order. If that doesn't suit your reading style, you should at least understand and keep in mind the overall framework of the stages and tactics to help you understand each concept in its proper context.

Each tactic we will cover in this book represents training for a role that you'll need to fill or a hat that you'll get to wear. The book and framework within are organized so that you understand how all of the roles in an early-stage venture tie together. As an entrepreneurial leader it is your job to coordinate how they operate, now and as the venture and team scale.

More generally, your job is not to do exactly what you read in this book. Instead, use the tactics and examples to craft your own experiments that will push your venture forward towards your mission and have the most impact possible.

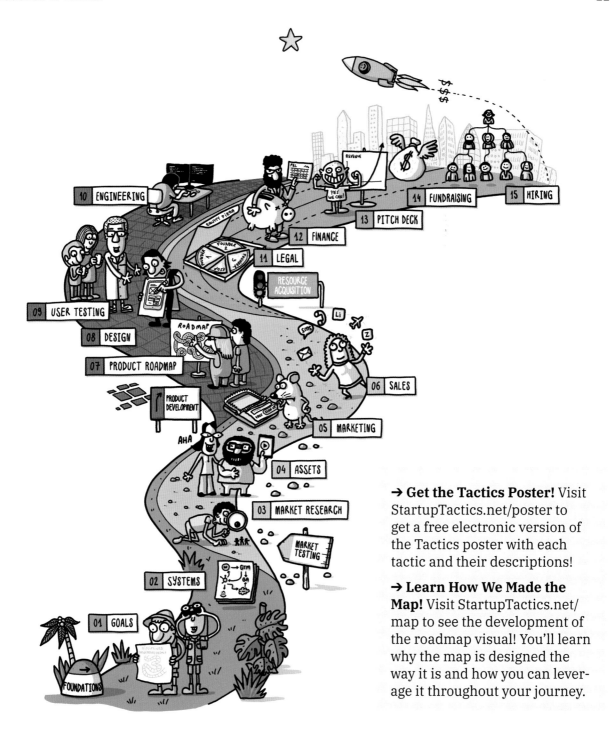

→ **Get the Tactics Poster!** Visit StartupTactics.net/poster to get a free electronic version of the Tactics poster with each tactic and their descriptions!

→ **Learn How We Made the Map!** Visit StartupTactics.net/map to see the development of the roadmap visual! You'll learn why the map is designed the way it is and how you can leverage it throughout your journey.

Output

This book isn't just theory and, if you apply it to your own venture, you won't come away empty-handed. If you read this book through, follow the exercises included, and apply each of these tactics to your new venture, you'll have a toolbox overflowing with valuable assets:

- Operational goals
- KPIs
- Project and file management tools
- CRM systems
- Payroll and finance tools
- Quantitative and qualitative primary research
- Website
- Social media presence
- Branding
- Logo
- Creative brief
- Marketing strategy
- Digital advertising campaigns
- Landing pages
- Sales pipeline
- Sales pitch
- Sales materials
- Lead generation techniques
- Product vision and strategy
- Product roadmap
- Prototypes
- User testing
- Minimum Viable Business Product (MVBP)

- Software architecture
- Development tools and technology
- Incorporation and legal documents
- Financial model
- Path to profitability
- Banking relationships
- Pitch deck
- Funding leads
- Organizational chart
- Recruiting plan
- New hire onboarding plan

You will surely feel more prepared to create a successful venture with all that in your back pocket.

WORKBOOK: PERSONAL SKILLS SCORECARD PRE-ASSESSMENT

Before you start learning the tactics, you should develop an understanding of where you stand in each of the functional skills that an entrepreneur needs. Start by rating your experience and comfort level with each of the tactical skills that an entrepreneur needs.

ADDITIONAL RESOURCES

→ **Download the Pre-Assessment Scorecard!** Visit StartupTactics.net/scorecard

At the end of this book I encourage you to reevaluate your skills in each area to see how much you have learned and where you need to sharpen skills through practice and application.

Foundations

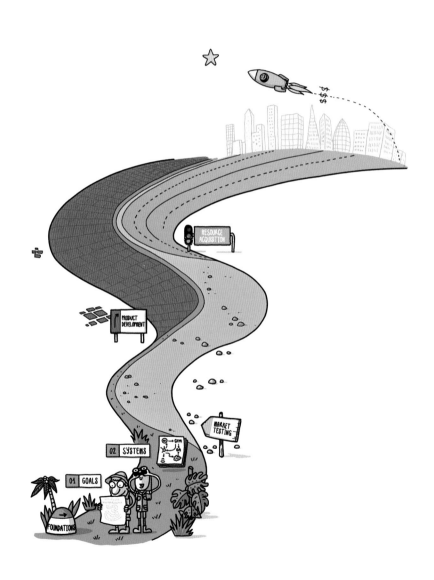

Before you begin building your business, you need to get your foundational structures in place. These early tactics will ensure you're focused on the right "things" because time is a precious resource so it's best not to waste it.

Tracking the things you and your team are doing will also help set you up for success in communicating the progress you've made when it comes time to explore Stage 4, Resource Acquisition. The better you can articulate what you said you were going to do, what you actually did, and what you are going to do next, the easier it becomes to get more money and, as a result, more time. A consistent theme throughout these tactics is doing the right things to unlock additional resources.

We start laying the foundations here, including the goals and systems you need to set up your business for success.

Goals

Operational Goals and KPIs—Charting the Course to Major Milestones

01 | GOALS

We're ready to dive into Tactic 1, goals. I do want to make sure, however, that you have the context working your way into this tactical framework. For that reason I would recommend that you read the introduction if you haven't done so already. Onward!

Goals give us structure, which supports our path to success. Defining strong goals may seem simple until you actually dig into it. Turning the wrong objective into your North Star could also doom your venture before it even gets started, so take this process seriously.

In This Tactic, You Will:

- Set goals for the venture that are derived from your vision for the future state of the world.
- Determine which metrics to track for each goal to stay on track.
- Build a process for checking in on your progress towards goals and reevaluating.

Breaking Down the Vision

As an entrepreneur, you have a vision of what the world looks like in the future and how you can improve it. This relates to your raison d'être. Take a few moments to think about what the world looks like in five to ten years with your new innovation-driven enterprise. How is it different from the world we live in right now?

Your entire team also needs to understand what your vision looks like. I regularly reference Linda Hill of Harvard Business School early on in my class while students are forming teams. In 2001, she published a paper that frames the team development process by saying, "A group of people working together does not automatically equal a team."[1]

THE ENTREPRENEURSHIP SUCCESS PIE

DISCIPLINED
ENTREPRENEURSHIP

REFER TO STEP

0

GETTING
STARTED

If we are to define a team, which we believe to be the most important part of any new entrepreneurial venture, it is a group with a common vision who are working towards a common goal. Aligning on the same vision leaves us with one other thing to align on: common goals. The vision will be the basis for the goals you set, both short-term and long-term.

I encourage you to sit in a quiet space and think this through before continuing on with the book. Take 30 minutes to explore your vision of the world. It will provide greater clarity during the next steps you take in executing your business plan.

[1] https://www.ugent.be/doctoralschools/en/doctoraltraining/courses/transferableskills/note-on-teams.pdf

Why New Ventures Need Goals

With limited runway, ambitious visions of the future state of the world, and the need to acquire more resources to continue working towards that vision, new ventures need to be sharply focused on what matters most. These goals not only keep the team locked in on the venture's priorities, but they also provide opportunities to hold each other accountable and keep yourselves on track.

There is a common misconception that entrepreneurs live unstructured lives. Many people believe entrepreneurs wake up whenever they want in the morning and work on whatever they feel like throughout the day, all on their own schedule. While there may be some truth to that flexibility, successful entrepreneurs—and all people for that matter—thrive in environments where they have structure. Creating and sticking to routines help individuals flourish.

Corporate roles provide structure. If you work a corporate job you have generally set hours (perhaps 9 a.m. to 5 p.m.), goals from your boss, and project timelines. The most successful entrepreneurs have to create a structure for themselves, although maybe not as constraining as they'd find in a big corporation.

There is a significant difference between being handed goals and creating them for yourself. In a corporate role, your boss will likely present goals to you. As an entrepreneur, you must set goals yourself—especially when first starting out. Later you will have the help and input of your investors and board.

Setting the Right Goals

There are a lot of things you could spend your time on. Prioritizing makes sure you invest your time in the things that will ultimately unlock additional resources, even if that means some other things do not get done. The unvarnished truth is that your business will not survive without additional resources, and if you don't set—and hit!—the right goals, you'll have a hard time acquiring them.

Everyone thinks that they're good at setting goals until the rubber meets the road and they write goals down on paper and then read them back. Sharing goals with your team, advisors, or other parties often reveals that goals perhaps lack clarity, aren't specific enough, or do not align with future milestones. Practice makes perfect.

Starting with your future vision of the world, you should work backward to define the milestones that will help you unlock those additional resources.

Ask yourself "What do I need to do to get more time and money?" You might not have the correct answer, so you need to validate you're on the right track and also ask that question of those who can eventually provide more resources for you. In many cases that might be investors or other funders, which we will explore more in Tactic 14.

Once you know what you need to do to unlock additional resources, break it down into shorter-term goals.

Methodologies

There are many goal-setting methodologies, such as SMART, WOOP, HARD, and others. Try different methodologies to determine which is the best fit for you and your business. Many startups that are at "day 0" and are just starting out will begin with a simple, straightforward goal-setting structure. Whether from the start or after some traction has been achieved, I recommend one option: objectives and key results (OKRs).

Originated by Andy Grove at Intel, OKRs are a method for goal setting derived from the "management by objectives theory" developed by Peter Drucker and presented in his book *Practice of Management*. John Doerr introduced it to Google's founders and discusses the topic in his book *Measure What Matters*. This approach combines objectives with key results to set management structure.

In your new venture, you must in some sense manage yourself along with your early team. This approach helps you to stay aligned with the team, track your progress towards hitting goals, and creates a bit of friendly competition. This is where OKRs come in handy. You can think of objectives and key results this way:

<u>O</u>bjectives are high-level goals that are achievable but not measurable.

> *Example: Confirm we have identified the correct Beachhead Market.*

DISCIPLINED ENTREPRENEURSHIP

REFER TO STEP

2

BEACHHEAD MARKET

<u>K</u>ey <u>R</u>esults are measurable milestones that contribute towards hitting an objective.

> *Examples:*
> *1. Validate with three sources that the size of the market segment is appropriate.*
> *2. Sign up 15 potential customers on our waitlist from the market segment.*
> *3. Gather feedback on our product design from five people in the segment.*

When implementing OKRs for your team, aim to have three to five objectives and three to five key results for each objective. Note that the objective is high-level while the key results are measurable and, when combined, achieve the objective. Also note that you won't find more discrete to-do list items or specific activities included.

Regardless of which structure you choose, review these goals with others and get feedback. You might choose to do this with co-founders, team members, advisors (formal or informal), your board, or investors. Their feedback will help you to refine and work towards the milestones that represent meaningful progress for the venture.

Tracking Goals with Metrics and KPIs

For each goal you set—regardless of which methodology you use—determine which metric or key performance indicator (KPI) you will use to track progress. In the context of OKRs, for example, you would have a metric associated with each of the key results since the objectives are not meant to be measurable. This metric will help you to understand whether you are on track to hit the goal, whether you already reached it, and whether you set goals with the appropriate amount of reach/challenge. You should make sure your goals are motivating to the team and present a challenge, but aren't so unrealistic they're unattainable.

These metrics will be the basis for the next tactic, Tactic 2, as the systems you select need to track these KPIs.

Value of Assigning Ownership

Together, the goals help to align priorities for the organization as a whole. For each goal you should have an individual owner. One person should be responsible for hitting each goal, providing individuals clarity in what their personal priorities are. One of the benefits of introducing such a structured approach to goal setting is that it serves as an accountability tool.

Assigning ownership also helps balance the team's workload. You may find you have gaps between your goals and the skillsets of your team. These gaps identify who else you may need to bring on board, either short-term or long-term, to ensure the venture's goals can be reached. We will explore hiring in greater detail in Tactic 15.

Accountability: Recurring Check-in Meetings

To make sure you hit your goals, schedule regularly recurring check-in meetings. Check-in meetings aren't just for large organizations. These check-in meetings help measure progress towards the top-priority goals, hold the owners for each goal accountable, and also provide opportunity to reassess goals.

Activities and To-Do Lists

Your goals are not to-dos. Each individual on the team should have a personal to-do list and the items on that list should be aligned with the short-term goals they own and are responsible for.

One of the most valuable exercises you can do on a regular basis is reviewing your to-do list and striking any activities that do not directly tie to an organization-level goal. If there is an activity you feel like you should be doing that doesn't directly tie to an existing organization-level goal, you may want to reevaluate.

Reevaluating at Regular Intervals and Resource Changes

Recently I sat down with a former student who was in the process of improving their team. They informed me that several part-time team members would be leaving or shifting to advisory roles and several new full-time team members were joining to take the venture to the next level. This exciting news was very welcome, but also necessitated the reevaluation of the organization's goals.

I asked the former student to grab a notebook and pencil, and then take some time away from the craziness of daily life. I proposed 30 minutes in a quiet room to restart the goal-setting process starting with a refresh of their future state of the world—their vision. I recommended this because a change to the team means a change in resources. The limited resources of a mostly part-time team were made slightly less limited with new full-time team members, creating much more bandwidth to get things done. With more time should come the ability to achieve more than was reasonable previously, but using that time wisely doesn't happen without intentionality.

Instead of simply reevaluating goals at the end of a month, quarter, or year, I recommend reviewing and revising goals whenever the business changes or there are changes in resources. More money or more time—or less money and time—means it's time for goal adjustments.

EXAMPLE

ReHome

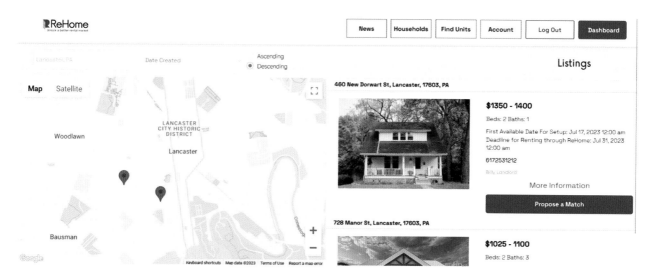

The ReHome platform highlights housing options for resettlement agencies.

Joe Landis is an entrepreneur on a mission. His raison d'être is to help with refugee resettlement. Recognizing that the United States is way behind on its refugee admissions targets, and that resettlement agencies on the ground report the biggest bottleneck is the nationwide lack of refugee-accessible housing, Landis set his sights on building a business to address these challenges. Landis began building a two-sided marketplace where resettlement agencies and landlords can find tenant matches according to resettlement-specialized criteria.

To advance his venture and work towards addressing the resettlement challenge, Landis and his co-founder, Thomas Nguyen, defined a set of objectives and key results for the next stage of the venture. Doing so helped the team to align on what they were working towards, provided clarity on what activities deserved time and energy, and introduced accountability with monthly goal check-ins. Landis reflected, "Without structure, it can be easy to be swept up in the many priorities that are important to ReHome's success. Writing these priorities down in clear categories and getting specific about the timeline has helped."

Over the timeframe of these OKRs, ReHome was able to accomplish the majority of the key results. Landis and his team rehashed the objectives with delayed results, like Objective 2, into a new OKR framework for the summer months that followed.

Objective 1	Piloting in Lancaster ready to run by June 1
Key Result 1	MOUs signed with two resettlement agencies (CWS Lancaster and Bethany Christian Services in Lancaster)
Key Result 2	Commitments from 20 landlords in Lancaster and 2 property management companies to list their units on the platform during the pilot
Key Result 3	3-5 key research questions set for Joe's thesis research, with strategic alignment to ReHome's strategy

Objective 2	Funding structure for business finalized in time to incorporate by June 1
Key Result 1	Develop and choose between 3 or more scenarios of cash flow and business development plans based on PMR
Key Result 2	Acquire at least one legal opinion and do thorough primary/secondary research on the types of government partnershps/funding structures available under nonprofit vs. profit-earning status
Key Result 3	Assess partnerships with MIT/Harvard resettlement research-action group, BU resettlement research node, and the national Refugee Housing Solutions technical assistance organization

Objective 3	Product MVP ready to launch in Lancaster by Late May
Key Result 1	Define top three features to be included on each side of the platform in order to reach 50% of potential landlords and full participation of Lancaster's two local agencies
Key Result 2	Create one or more versions of each feature for use during the pilot
Key Result 3	Secure website and any other digital tools that are necessary for the MVP

Objective 4	Better understanding of post-beachhead markets
Key Result 1	Estimate the TAM of the entire US resettlement-based housing market based on real data from RAs
Key Result 2	Create an overview of current matching practices within the resettlement-based housing market.
Key Result 3	Determine whether to include community sponsorship groups as a second group on the Demand side of the market alongside RAs (note: this will involve more PMR with RAs and an analysis of the size of that potential market)

Objective 5	Funding secured to continue ramp-up of ReHome through Dec 2023
Key Result 1	Raise $10K in minimally-restricted funds by June 1 (from Sandbox, potential foundation donors, ...)
Key Result 2	Pitch ReHome to 5-10 potential grant funders
Key Result 3	Successful application to delta v

Summary

In order to advance your venture towards your vision, you need to have a rigorous approach to goal setting. You should set goals, determine which metrics to track for each goal, assign an owner from your team, and check in on a routine basis to make sure that you are on track to hit your goals. As you move forward you should question whether tasks on your to-do list, or the ways you spend your limited time, are actually contributing towards your goals. The goals you set here in Tactic 1 will help you determine how and when to apply subsequent tactics.

TOOLS OF THE TRADE

Google Sheets (google.com/sheets)

Monday.com (Monday.com)

Asana (asana.com)

Notion (notion.so)

Weekdone (weekdone.com)

Todoist (todoist.com/home)

Profit.co (profit.co)

Trakstar (trakstar.com)

ClickUp (clickup.com)

Quantive (quantive.com)

PROMPTS

1. Determine where you would like to be as a business overall in three to six months.

2. Outline your month-by-month high-level technical and business milestones.

3. Fill in some of the blanks on the OKR template to chart your course:

   a. Determine high-level objectives.

   b. Outline key results to achieve the objectives.

   c. Identify and assign activities for each KR.

4. Identify which key metrics will be necessary to track for your OKRs.

5. Schedule recurring meetings (if you don't already have them) and set up running agenda notes for each of your recurring meetings.

WORKBOOK

Get the Startup Tactics Goal Setting Workbook, which will help you to align on the next steps for your venture to achieve the milestones needed to achieve your mission. Within you will find worksheets that include:

1. Time Horizon: You must determine, as a team, the time horizon for your goals.
2. Goals: Once you are aligned on a time horizon, you need to define your goals.
3. KPIs: You'll need metrics to track your progress towards your goals.
4. Owners: You and your teammates should take ownership of each goal.
5. Check-ins: To stay on track, you will define a plan to regularly check in on your goals.
6. Early-Stage Goals: For early startups, this framework provides an alternative approach.

ADDITIONAL RESOURCES

→ **Get the Workbook!** Visit StartupTactics.net/goals

Systems

Startup Tooling and Systems

02 SYSTEMS

New ventures need easy-to-use, flexible tools and systems, but—unlike larger, established organizations—they don't need every system under the sun. Determining what needs to be in place when and planning accordingly begins early in a venture's existence, but anticipating new needs and reevaluating current solutions should occur on a regular basis.

In This Tactic, You Will:

- Determine which systems you will ultimately need as a business.
- Prioritize the systems you need based on the goals you set in Tactic 1.
- Try tools that you and your team will align on using to maximize efficiency.

Goals Are Only as Good as the Systems

We can set the best goals in the world, but unless we hit them we are not advancing the venture. How do we know whether we're on track to hit a goal? How can we prove we reached it? Metrics and KPIs help us define and track our success for each goal, but we need tools and systems to monitor and bring visibility to our progress.

Must-Have Systems for Startups

Like any organization, startups and new ventures eventually need a variety of different systems, including CRM (customer relationship management), file management, project management, finance and accounting, payroll, expense management, and business intelligence. The question we must ask is which systems does a startup need *right now*?

If we think about day 0 startups, it's safe to assume they likely don't require an advanced accounting system. In fact, advanced accounting systems require extensive training and configuration, which will simply be a drain on our precious resources.

To determine which systems a startup needs *right now* simply refer back to the current goals and associated metrics. For each goal's metric, determine which system is required to track the progress toward that metric. For example, if a goal is building a customer waitlist and the success metric is 300 individuals on said waitlist, then a CRM is likely a system we need early on.

Finding Flexibility: Startup versus Corporate Tools and Systems

We can't use just any CRM system as a day 0 startup. We may be more familiar with Salesforce or Oracle NetSuite from previous roles in larger, established organizations, but they're overkill and prohibitively expensive for a new venture. Like complex accounting software, these tools will require extensive configuration and training for others on the team, which will also drain resources. We also don't yet necessarily know exactly how our business will work. Business processes will evolve and the metrics we're following remain dynamic since they are based on our short-term goals.

Any subsequent changes in the metrics reporting or alterations to the processes in the system will take significantly more time and money with enterprise-grade systems. You can evaluate whether a system is fit for a new venture by measuring the amount of time required to make a change. Literally, grab a stopwatch. It if takes more than 60 seconds to make a simple change, such as adding a new field to track information, it might not be a fit for your early-stage, rapidly evolving venture. Small configuration changes might take hours in a complex system designed for large organizations, so avoid draining resources on these poor fits and opt for systems best suited for a rapidly changing business.

Keeping It Simple

Before you have a firm grasp on the business you're building, you should seek out the simplest systems to make sure everyone uses them. For communication and documentation in the early days, Nikita Bier, the founder of Gas and TBH, believes the productivity stack should be nothing more than "an iMessage thread and a single Apple Note."[1] While iMessage and Apple Notes might not be the exact platforms you and your team use, the concept of building with systems that everyone already uses is powerful.

The simplest, cheapest system out there once you're ready to track progress towards metrics and KPIs? A spreadsheet. We can spend an incredible amount of time selecting new systems, wasting days "playing" with systems to learn how they work. But the simplest accounting system is a spreadsheet, and in the first year of a new venture it *might* be enough to handle all your current reporting requirements. Often, starting with a spreadsheet for each of your goal's metrics gets you enough experience and knowledge to better understand the systems you need moving forward.

Planned Obsolescence

Planned obsolescence means designing something not intended to last. It is quite common in consumer products, which are designed to have a specific lifetime. While their motivation might be to prompt the customer to purchase another version once the old one can't cut it, we're adopting this mindset so we can stay scrappy!

---

[1] https://twitter.com/nikitabier/status/1621577684609536000

A spreadsheet might be suitable now, but it will be frowned upon in an IPO process. Accepting that you'll need to upgrade at some point down the line but that a spreadsheet gets the job done today is a sign of healthy resource prioritization. You can use a spreadsheet today, even knowing that it won't last beyond your next round of goal setting.

When your CRM needs outgrow the capabilities of a spreadsheet, you can then transition to a tool like Airtable. Once you outgrow Airtable you might graduate to Pipedrive or HubSpot. And eventually it's possible you will outgrow Pipedrive or HubSpot and graduate to Salesforce or Net-Suite. These transitions are expected as a business grows. Plan for those eventualities but start with the most easily flexible tool to quickly and inexpensively mold the system to your business as it changes, which it will!

Signs It's Time to Transition

With the planned obsolescence approach you will need to be on the lookout for warning signs that it is time to transition. Getting ahead of this will make it as smooth and painless as possible for the team. Signs that it is time to transition include:

- Complex business processes no longer supported by simple systems
- Privacy settings limiting the control over potentially sensitive information
- Number of employees exceeds what can be supported by current systems
- Growing number of customers demand what systems can't support
- Increasing security concerns regarding the organization's information
- Regulatory review requires more advanced systems

Avoid Overinvesting in Trials

You could spend days, weeks, and months test-driving tools to find those that will be the best fit for the organization. And many people overinvest their precious time in trying lots of different tools and systems to make sure they have the "perfect" one. The reality is that the systems you start with don't need to be perfect. If you're on a day 0 hunt for a system that must absolutely accommodate an incredibly complex business process then you have likely over-engineered the business process already.

Applying Metcalfe's Law: Building Alignment on Tools and Systems Among Your Team

Metcalfe's law states that the value of a network is proportional to the square of the number of nodes in the network. You and your team, each a node on your network, should all be on the same network, your systems, to increase the value you can create.

Aside from choosing simple systems for tracking metrics for each of your goals, a fundamental element of startup systems is ensuring the team is aligned. While this might seem simple, teams not aligned on the systems they are investing in become immediately inefficient. For example, a team that does not have basic alignment on the file-sharing system they are using is hampering each individual's ability to easily find the information they need to advance the venture.

EXAMPLE

Oceanworks

Oceanworks began with the goal of reducing plastic pollution in our oceans through the commercial sale of recycled ocean plastic. In the early days we employed Salesforce as a system to help track progress towards goals set related to the number of new customers.

As a new business, there was still much to learn about the target customer and ideal sales process to acquire those customers. Through a series of experiments we determined that selling samples of recycled ocean plastic would allow us to collect information and build long-term customer relationships. Using Salesforce allowed us to track all of the information about customers, their needs, and associated order information.

Salesforce quickly became problematic because it took too long to navigate the system, collect different types of information about customers and objections they had, and customize the software to meet the sales process we were testing. As the sales process evolved there was routinely not enough time to customize the system to meet the business needs. Not to mention, there was a large expense for a system as robust as Salesforce. A perfect fit for a well-established business, Salesforce did not suit the needs of Oceanworks at the time.

We decided to simplify and shifted the business operations to Airtable. With Airtable, anyone on the team could make changes to the information systems, including adding fields and configuring the database just as if it was a spreadsheet. No longer was a trained Salesforce consultant needed. It was clear that Airtable was not going to be a long-term solution, but that in the short term it would enable the team to track progress towards company-level goals and for the company's systems to evolve more quickly, aligned with the rate of change of the business processes. This change saved tens of thousands of dollars and a significant amount of time, allowing the team to focus on advancing the business.

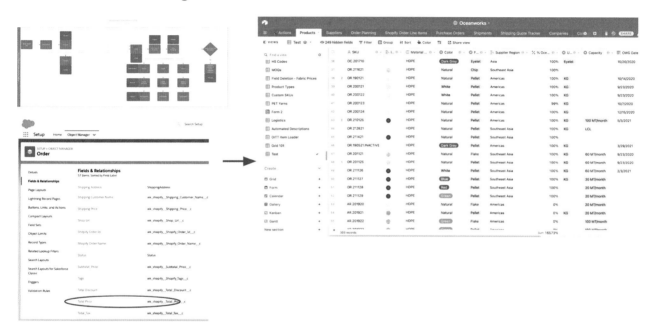

The complex Salesforce implementation was transitioned to Airtable for flexibility as the Oceanworks business model evolved.

Summary

Every business needs a suite of systems to operate across each of the functions, including sales, finance, human resources, and so on. You will need these too, eventually. To start you need the systems that are going to collect the information needed to track progress towards your goals. Some additional tools may be needed for your team's productivity and everyone on the teams should be aligned on what these are. Over time, the systems you put in place will become less flexible. For now, flexibility allows you to adapt systems to meet the rapidly changing business needs.

TOOLS OF THE TRADE

Any System

Google Sheets (sheets.google.com)

Project Management

Monday.com (monday.com)

Asana (asana.com)

Notion (notion.so)

Email

Google Workspace (workspace.google.com)

Microsoft Office (office.com)

Superhuman (superhuman.com)

Communication

Slack (slack.com)

Meta Workspace (about.meta.com/technologies/workplace)

Microsoft Teams (microsoft.com/en-us/microsoft-teams/group-chat-software)

Google Chat (workspace.google.com/products/chat)

Discord (discord.com)

Documents and File Management

Google Drive (drive.google.com)

Microsoft Office (office.com)

Dropbox (dropbox.com)

Box (box.com)

Notion (notion.so)

Coda (coda.io)

CRM

HubSpot (hubspot.com)

Pipedrive (pipedrive.com)

Salesforce (salesforce.com)

Finance

QuickBooks (quickbooks.com)

Freshbooks (freshbooks.com)

Xero (xero.com)

Payroll

Gusto (gusto.com)

Deel (deel.com)

TriNet (trinet.com)

Paychex (paychex.com)

PROMPTS

1. Determine which systems you'll need for the next three to six months.

2. Sign up for and set up/configure the systems you'll need to rely on.

3. Evaluate whether the systems you have now will track your progress towards the goals and metrics that you defined for your startup last week.

4. Design an "accounting system" for your team for the next three months.

5. If you already have some systems set up, define what you plan to expand:

   a. What tools might you transition to?

   b. When will be the right time to transition?

6. Try signing up for three tools/systems that you expect you might need in the next three to six months and evaluate whether they will be flexible enough.

WORKBOOK

Get the Startup Tactics Systems Workbook, which will help you to align on the next steps for your venture to achieve the milestones needed to achieve your mission. Within you will find worksheets that include:

1. Core Systems: Decide on tools and systems you'll use as a team outside of your KPIs.
2. Tools and Systems Evaluation: Start by identifying tools and systems you could use.
3. KPI to System Matching: Identify the right system for each of your KPIs.
4. Evolution of Systems: Determine how you might transition to other systems over time.

ADDITIONAL RESOURCES

→ **Get the Workbook!** Visit StartupTactics.net/systems

Market Testing

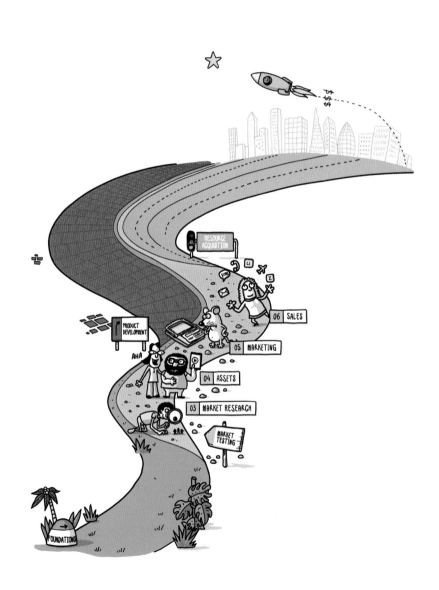

With your venture's foundations now established through goal setting and startup systems, you are prepared to pursue market testing. Market testing helps you validate not just that your hypothesized target customer wants your quantified value proposition, but also helps you actually refine your End User Profile, Persona, Full Life Cycle Use Case, Quantified Value Proposition, and High-Level Product Specification.

Market testing begins with a continuation of any market research you've already begun. A combination of brief secondary market research and extensive primary market research will position you with relevant knowledge about the market in which you are going to test. This knowledge will help you design the most insightful tests that produce unique insights others don't have access to. Following market research comes the development of startup assets. These assets are digital and lightweight. They include, but are not limited to, a simple website, logo, and any graphics or videos that clearly and concisely communicate the value your venture proposes to provide.

DISCIPLINED ENTREPRENEURSHIP

REFER TO STEP

3

END USER PROFILE

REFER TO STEP

5

BEACHHEAD PERSONA

REFER TO STEP

6

LIFE CYCLE USE CASE

REFER TO STEP

8

QUANTIFIED VALUE PROP

DISCIPLINED
ENTREPRENEURSHIP

REFER TO STEP
9
FIRST 10
CUSTOMERS

REFER TO STEP
8
QUANTIFIED
VALUE PROP

REFER TO STEP
12
DECISION
MAKING UNIT

These assets are then put to the test in the real world. First, through marketing with extremely narrow targeting towards your end users, or several different hypothesized end-user segments. This tactic helps you to build the top of your customer funnel and build an understanding of whether your end user actually wants the quantified value proposition that your market research suggests they do. Subsequently, market testing includes outbound sales. This tactic addresses how to build a lead list of high qualified potential customer targets and compose outreach campaigns.

Market testing takes place before the other stages because, as an entrepreneur, your two most precious resources are time and money. Without maximizing how you use those, your business fails. This book is designed to help you acquire additional resources, and your best odds of acquiring additional resources come by building conviction in others.

Consider how you can leverage market testing tactics to evaluate interest from different members of your decision-making unit (DMU). For example, if building a marketplace you might choose to employ the marketing tactic to target your end users and the sales tactic to target your economic buyers.

Investing your energy in high-quality market testing before proceeding with product development and further resource acquisition helps ensure you are building the right product for the right customer. As you proceed through market testing your goal is data collection. You will benefit greatly from having data to speak to, metrics related to PMR insights, marketing campaigns, and sales outreach responses. It will result in a list of potential customers who want the solution you're proposing to build.

You can then leverage this list of real customers to build both the personal conviction to move forward with product development and the conviction for others who can provide additional resources. But this only happens if you propose to build something that creates real value, which this stage should confirm either way.

Market Research

Advanced Primary and Secondary Market Research—Quantifying Qualitative Research

03 | MARKET RESEARCH

You hopefully haven't gotten this far into your venture without having lots of conversations with potential customers and prospects. Without this baseline understanding of the problems and pain points that customers face, it's nearly impossible to deliver a solution that truly satisfies customer needs.

But these anecdotal observations aren't enough to justify major strategic decisions. The strongest founders quantify the insights from their primary market research (PMR) to build conviction in themselves and others that they have found the origin of a new venture.

In This Tactic, You Will:

- Build a process for conducting primary market research that incorporates qualitative research including interviews, observation, and immersion.

- Find and reach out to people who match your End User Profile to conduct interviews.

- Quantify your qualitative primary market research findings to communicate insights with data.

- Expand upon your qualitative research with quantitative surveying techniques.

PMR Never Ends

PMR is an entrepreneurial skill that allows us to get to know our customers just as well as we know our best friends. Much as you need to continue investing in friendships, you need to also keep investing in your PMR. Building on the basics of PMR outlined in *Disciplined Entrepreneurship*, we will explore some advanced tactics to most efficiently and effectively conduct PMR.

Focus on Qualitative PMR

When you begin conducting PMR, you need to remain in inquiry mode, starting with qualitative research that asks open-ended questions. Based on what you learn from these sessions, you can separate the trends and commonalities from the oddities and exceptions of a particular research subject. Broadening the pool of research subjects diffuses potential biases from one or two customers from skewing your entire view of the market.

Qualitative PMR should not be limited exclusively to interviews, because a combination of interviewing, observation, and immersion will help you to best understand the priorities of your end users. User testing is another helpful form of qualitative PMR, but by definition exists in advocacy mode, not inquiry mode. For that reason, we will revisit user testing in Tactic 9, User Testing: Validating the Product *Actually* Works.

You can then transition to quantitative PMR, specifically surveys (covered later in this tactic), where you'll work to confirm the hypotheses and assumptions from qualitative sessions across a broader cohort of potential customers.

Putting the Process in Place

The primary market research process is one that will require a significant time investment, and it is a garbage-in, garbage-out process. A structured approach will help to ensure that you are always investing your time in disproving your hypotheses. A general guide you can follow looks like this:

1. Articulate three to five hypotheses to be tested.
2. Define qualifications for research subjects.
3. Make a list of potential PMR subjects to reach out to.
4. Ask for a meeting or call.

5. Talk to them face to face if possible, via video chat if not.

6. Interpret results, adjust hypotheses, and repeat.

Maintaining Your Pool of Participants

Just as you should reach out to your best friends on a regular basis to keep the connection fresh, you need to do the same with your PMR participants. Keeping up the relationship and continuing to update them on your progress further sets the stage for them to become your first paying customers.

As your business evolves, you will develop new hypotheses and key assumptions needing validation through testing. Your PMR participants will be crucial to quickly disproving or confirming these hypotheses.

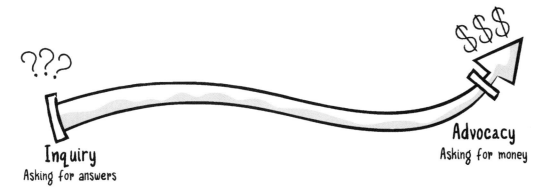

Inquiry
Asking for answers

Advocacy
Asking for money

DISCIPLINED
ENTREPRENEURSHIP

REFER TO STEP

20

KEY ASSUMPTION
IDENTIFICATION

REFER TO STEP

22

minimum viable
BUSINESS PRODUCT

Your transition from inquiry mode to advocacy mode relies on small rapid iterations as you develop from an idea to a high-level product specification, low-fidelity mockup, high-fidelity mockup, minimum viable business product, and ultimately a polished product. Each iteration will likely have multiple versions that, when combined, lead to advocacy mode.

Expanding Your Pool of Participants

As the business grows and matures you will need to recruit additional individuals to participate in quantitative and qualitative research activities. These new voices will

DISCIPLINED
ENTREPRENEURSHIP

REFER TO STEP
2
BEACHHEAD
MARKET

REFER TO STEP
3
END USER
PROFILE

REFER TO STEP
5
BEACHHEAD
PERSONA

REFER TO STEP
12
DECISION
MAKING UNIT

expand your learnings and provide you with fresh input from people who do not yet have context, and resulting bias, which will impact your insights.

As your business evolves you will also gain more clarity about who your end user really is, which often disqualifies some of your existing pool of participants. For example, if your solution was originally targeted for manufacturing firms but market research revealed that you really should focus further up the supply chain on materials providers, those manufacturer interview subjects can get dropped from the cohort. At this point you may need to update your End User Profile and Persona to ensure this shift in focus is reflected in your team's ongoing research.

As you further home in on who your end user is, you will also begin investigating the other decision-makers and stakeholders intrinsic to closing deals and ensuring the product meets everyone's needs. You'll want to add individuals matching these other profiles to your PMR activities.

Begin by going back to your existing pool of participants and asking the individuals who most closely match your End User Profile for referrals to others who share similar characteristics. You will also want to go back to the watering holes—physical and digital places where your end users gather together—that you have already identified. However, you may also need to identify additional watering holes.

Virtual Watering Holes

Introduction to Virtual Watering Holes

Watering holes are places where you can find a large number of similar people within your Beachhead Market to conduct PMR. For example, at the Aviation Engineering Association annual meeting, you will likely find a large number of aerospace engineers with whom you can conduct PMR if you're building a product for next-generation passenger jets.

However, not every target market has a meeting every year where they all gather. It's often not possible or feasible to find a large number of your target customers in a single place. Perhaps these individuals do not congregate together regularly, the events are too far and costly to get to from your home base, or admission is too expensive or not allowed. To deal with this dearth of PMR subjects, explore the concept of a virtual watering hole.

Virtual watering holes can help you to find more people matching your End User Profile at the lowest possible price point. Virtual watering holes are similar to their physical counterparts in that they are communities with many members who share the same demographics and psychographics as your target end users.

Finding Virtual Watering Holes

The specifics of your target market will dictate the degree of difficulty in locating these spaces. For example, if you are looking to develop products for new mothers, you can search for communities with many new mothers in them, such as on Meta's platform, Facebook.

A search on Facebook for "new mothers" groups.

A quick search reveals hundreds of groups on the social media platform filled with new and expecting mothers. The first result is a group of 4,700 individuals. While all 4,700 individuals aren't necessarily an exact match for all your target demographics and psychographics, it provides a starting point. Within the group, you might choose to segment the members, or you might choose to identify other, more targeted groups.

Another example, if you're ramping up a B2B business with Chief Information Security Officer (CISO) as your target customer title, you can search LinkedIn for groups using the "ciso" search term. This search reveals 479 different groups.

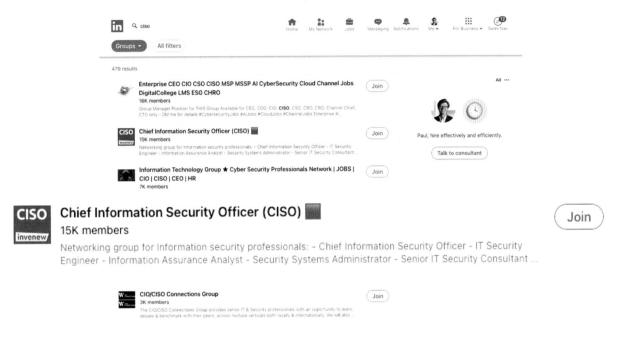

This LinkedIn search reveals 479 groups with the "CISO" keyword.

An alternate approach might be targeting individuals based on proxy products from your End User Profile. For example, if you know your target customers also use Affirm, a buy-now-pay-later finance tool for consumers, then you can explore Affirm's Facebook page.

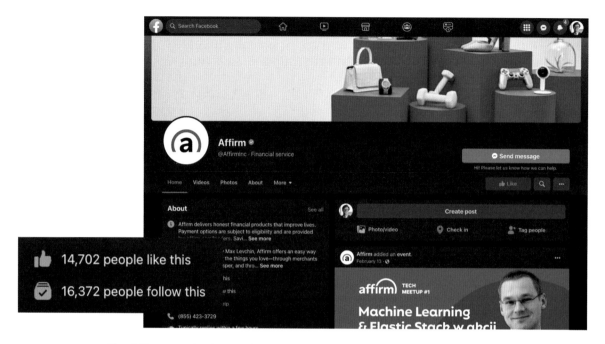

The Affirm Facebook page has about 14,700 likes and 16,300 followers.

On this page you can easily find those who follow or like the page and are engaged by clicking into any of the posts to see who liked or commented. Similar to the new mothers group, we need to assume that not everyone who follows Affirm fits our End User Profile, but the group of individuals serves as a starting point.

When You Can't Find a Virtual Watering Hole

Some target customers are nearly impossible to find either in person or online. Virtual watering holes might help, but be prepared with advanced approaches to identifying the right online communities and locations where they're active. One student who was having trouble finding a virtual watering hole told me:

> *Unfortunately, I couldn't find any online watering holes for social media platform misinformation policy teams (there are plenty for fact-checkers/people in the larger disinformation space, but they're not the ones making those decisions at Facebook/TikTok/etc.). I think they mainly keep their conversations private since what they do would be highly confidential.*

How do we find such a seemingly elusive virtual watering hole? In this example, it makes sense that we might struggle to find watering holes for social media misinformation policy teams. To start, we went to the source: our Persona. We began by finding an example of this Persona on LinkedIn. As of June 2023, Ella Irwin was the leader for product and trust at Twitter (now known as X). Looking at Ella's professional experience we know she also held similar trust and safety roles at a variety of technology companies and is a clear fit for the End User Profile.

Now we want to know where she spends time online. To find these watering holes we scrolled down to the bottom of Ella's profile to the "Interests" section and chose the "Groups" tab to see the groups she is a part of.

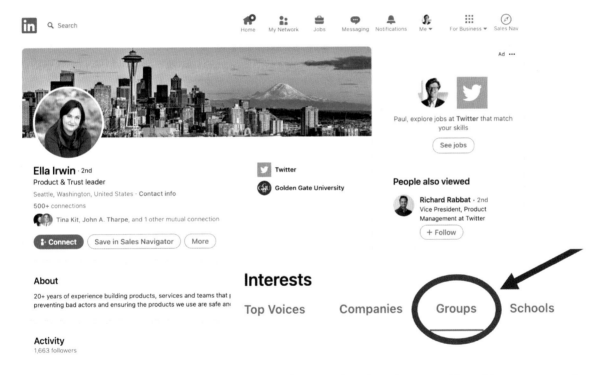

Ella Irwin is the VP of Product, Trust & Safety at Twitter (now known as X), and her groups can be found in the "Interests" section of her LinkedIn profile.

After exploring her list of groups, we remained stumped by the lack of relevant groups and the absence of a viable virtual watering hole.

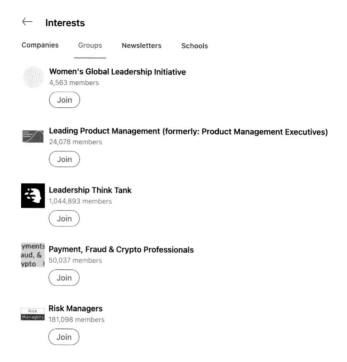

The groups that Ella is a member of on LinkedIn are not specific enough to social media trust.

To continue our hunt for virtual watering holes we leveraged the "People also viewed" list of similar profiles on LinkedIn and found another individual on Ella's team named Matthew.

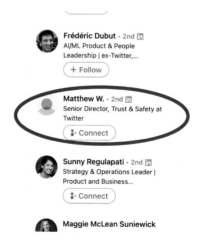

People who viewed Ella's profile also viewed Matthew.

DISCIPLINED
ENTREPRENEURSHIP

REFER TO STEP

12

DECISION
MAKING UNIT

It is important to note that Matthew does not have the same job title as Ella. While she is the vice president, he is a senior director. This difference is important because they likely play different roles in the decision-making unit (DMU). For PMR, we would start with the end user and maintain that focus for early-stage PMR. Regardless of this difference, the groups Matthew belongs to may lead to others who are potential end users.

The same was true of Matthew—he did not have any relevant groups that could be viable virtual watering holes. However, on his profile, we saw another director-level colleague, Keene Tso, who did lead us to potential virtual watering holes.

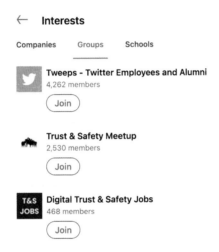

Keene Tso, a Director of Trust & Safety at Twitter (now known as X), was a member of two relevant LinkedIn groups that could serve as virtual watering holes.

The relevant groups where Keene was a member included more than 2,500 individuals also interested in trust and safety, many of whom would be relevant for PMR.

Outreach in Virtual Watering Holes

After identifying these virtual watering holes, next identify the individuals who would be the best fit for you to interview or observe for PMR. Rather than simply posting to the entire group, it is a stronger approach to reach out to more targeted individuals. This approach will:

- Allow you to conduct PMR with individuals who you already verified match other characteristics described in your End User Profile
- Increase the odds of scheduling time with the person you're reaching out to because you can send a personalized message more likely to resonate
- Reduce the risk you are kicked out of the group

Similar to a physical watering hole, you can expect a limited response rate. In an online watering hole, your response rate is likely to be even lower, so you may need to increase the amount of outreach communications you send.

Network Effects and Warm Introductions

When reaching out to potential customers to conduct PMR, it is important to consider how you can leverage your existing network to accelerate your progress towards speaking with customers in your target End User Profile. All else being equal, people are more likely to respond to you if they see that you are in their network. Before conducting PMR on a new End User Profile in a virtual watering hole such as Facebook or LinkedIn, you should first search through your connections on that platform. If you have first- or second-degree connections with people who are good candidates for PMR, you may want to contact them first before reaching out to others with whom you have not yet established a relationship. Keep in mind that there may be bias introduced should you conduct PMR with first-degree connections.

Warm introductions from people who are connected with customers you are targeting for PMR can be a big time saver. Think about who can introduce you to people in your market, and ask them for ideas on whom you can speak with. As you conduct more interviews over time, often the best way to find warm introductions is by asking the interviewees themselves whether they know anyone else who is experiencing the same pain points you discussed. Especially if you have discussed a problem that is important to them, you may find them willing to introduce you to their friends or colleagues. Remember, you have the potential to help them with the solution you are building, so it is in their interest for them to support you on your journey.

Moving Forward with Virtual Watering Holes

Virtual watering holes make you more efficient with your PMR outreach efforts to maximize your available resources. As you learn more about your target customer, you may need to move onto new virtual watering holes where more of those individuals interact online. Once you find a target customer who sticks, revisit the virtual watering holes where you found them and search for additional ones with similar traits to find new sources of input from your end users and potentially others in the decision-making unit.

Optimizing Outreach with Experiments

Much like the other tactics we will explore, experimentation is critical. When conducting outreach to individuals for PMR purposes, you should experiment with different watering holes and try out different messages to garner responses. One former student was conducting early research for Carestry, a company aimed at helping the 53 million adult Americans providing care for loved ones. His PMR outreach experiment yielded impressive results:

Hello, I'm John, a current MIT graduate student working on a class project that is focused on finding solutions to help caregivers. We think that by sharing your experience, we may find solutions to the situations that you and other caregivers are facing. I saw an old post of yours in a Caregiving support group, so I was hoping to connect with you for a short conversation. Please let me know if you would be willing. Thank you, John

0/14 Responses on Reddit and FB

Hi Emily, I wanted to introduce myself as we are in some similar groups, but more importantly it seems like we have a shared experience in family caregiving. I lost my father 4 years ago to pancreatic cancer and since then I have been trying to find ways to help people who are caregiving for a loved one. I am currently in grad school at MIT and am trying to speak to as many people as possible who are caregiving to try to fully understand the pain points. Would you be willing to have a short chat at some point about your experience?

60% Response Rate, 20% Convert to Call

You'll notice the more effective outreach features a more personal opening, clear intent, and a question at the end. By experimenting with various outreach messages, John could build a much stronger pool of PMR participants.

When It's Difficult to Find PMR Subjects

Take pause when you struggle to find participants for your primary market research, especially as you seek to expand your pool of participants. If you can't find *any* participants then you likely need to reevaluate your watering hole selection. If, however, you have found some primary market research participants and have difficulty identifying more then you should, take this as a sign. In this situation you have foresight into what your customer acquisition process will look like. It will be difficult, which isn't necessarily a dealbreaker, but should prompt reflection. Once you have identified some participants who share a common problem, they *should* be very happy and willing to introduce you to others.

Interviewing

Once you have your primary market research subjects committed to an interview, it's a good idea to prepare in advance. Going into the interview, you should have a predetermined list of questions that you would like to ask. As you build your "script" (this is in quotes because you are treating it as a conversation and not a script-reading exercise), you should consider whether any of the questions you ask might introduce bias into the conversation. You should also share the script you've built with a co-founder, advisor, or peer and ask them to analyze areas where bias could be introduced.

A potential script, or interview guide, might look like this:

0–3 minutes: Hello and introductions, get comfortable.

3–8 minutes: Ask the research subject about their world (as it relates to personal life, work life, etc. based on your hypotheses).

8–16 minutes: Ask them what could be improved, including a list of specific questions you have.

16–19 minutes: Ask for referrals to others who share similar End User Profile characteristics.

19–20 minutes: Thank them profusely, and leave. Follow up afterward.

You'll notice that nowhere in the script is a description of the product or solution that you envision. That would shift too far towards advocacy when early primary market research should aim to simply understand the problem and pain point.

The conversation will likely stray from the script you've prepared and that's okay. It should, because from the deviations you will likely learn new insights that will help you to revise your

hypotheses. However, to ensure consistency among your other interviews, you will want to be sure that you bring the conversation back to the questions you prepared.

Much like a reporter would interview a subject matter expert for an article or a salesperson would conduct a discovery call with a potential customer, your job is to ask questions, listen, and write notes. Your job is not to talk otherwise. Your research subject should do 90% of the talking.

Observational PMR

You'll get a ton of value from your conversations and interviews, but there's also value in not saying anything at all. As a complement to other PMR methods, try to find a willing participant or two (or more!) will allow you to shadow them. Depending on the nature of your product, this observation might last only a short while or could involve you following someone around for days. But regardless of the duration, the goal is to simply watch a sample end user in their natural environment performing whatever tasks your solution aims to address.

Try not to interrupt and ask too many questions; instead, take notes and debrief with them when it's over. It is, however, helpful to have them narrate what it is they're doing so you understand the context, their intent, and where they're getting frustrated.

You'll come away with a new appreciation for the challenges end users face, the impact of environmental factors, and probably a few new ideas for your product's feature set and your messaging. You will also now have a baseline of how things worked "before" your solution, which can be useful when creating success metrics and benchmarks.

Immersive PMR

You've asked lots of questions and made keen observations, but there's nothing like walking a mile in your customers' shoes to truly appreciate their predicament. That's why you should try to the best of your abilities to spend a day or so the same way they do.

This exercise in immersion should include you trying all the products they currently use to accomplish key tasks so you can fully appreciate the experience. Beyond that, you can engage with competitors to see what their sales process looks like and how they pitch their value proposition, cherry-picking what works and avoiding what doesn't when designing your own customer journey.

This immersive competitive intelligence gathering should also make a pit stop in their support forums, where you can both see how they respond to customer issues while also inventorying what seem to be common complaints. Finally, you can contact customer support for these products to get a full picture of the entire customer experience.

Spending a little time playing the role of a customer obviously isn't the same experience as doing it day after day, but it's yet another lens through which to view pain points and value propositions.

Keeping Records and Taking Notes

DISCIPLINED
ENTREPRENEURSHIP

REFER TO STEP

2

BEACHHEAD
MARKET

As you conduct PMR with your potential customers, it's important to carefully document what you learn in each meeting. The outcomes of each interview you perform will become the basis of a larger data set that you will mine for insights, and the quality of the data you collect will heavily impact your ability to find answers to your questions. It's not uncommon for founders to interview tens or even hundreds of potential customers before finalizing the selection of their Beachhead Market. By carefully thinking through what sort of information you will collect and how you collect it, you can greatly improve your ability to make well-informed decisions with the data you have on hand.

Here are a few guidelines that will help you generate a robust data pipeline from your PMR:

- Be ready to take notes during the interview, ideally electronically using a tool like Google Docs, Notion, or Coda. You'll see in the next section how a systematic approach to documenting your learnings will help to quantify the insights.

- List the questions you intend to ask alongside the hypotheses you are testing in the same document that you are using to take notes.

- Bring two team members to each interview. One team member should be fully engaged in the conversation, asking questions and interacting with the interviewee. The other team member should be mainly listening, observing, and taking notes.

- If possible, record audio using a tool that will generate a text transcript. This will enable you to catch points that are made quickly and reexamine them after the interview. Tools you can consider for this purpose are Otter, Fireflies, and Grain. Make sure to get permission from your interviewee before you start recording and keep in mind the potential for bias when interviewees know that they are being recorded.

- Immediately after each interview, talk with your teammate about what you heard and confirm your agreement on the result. Note whether each hypothesis was validated or invalidated.

- Finally, write three to five bullet points summarizing the key takeaways from the interview. In addition to your hypothesis validations, this might include new or unexpected points that you discovered. By keeping it short, you will make it easier to skim through this result alongside other interviews in the future.

- Move the three to five bullet points to a consolidated document that contains the findings from each of your PMR sessions in one place.

Quantifying Qualitative Research

I often hear from entrepreneurs who say they have spoken to X number of people and have a new subjective insight. In many cases, this isn't enough to build conviction in others that a new, unique insight has been validated. Entrepreneurs need data to convince others but too often jump from qualitative PMR to quantitative PMR prematurely to find the magic numbers that prove their hypotheses. There exists an interim step before quantitative research through which entrepreneurs can track their findings through not just written notes, but tallies and ratings for each individual they speak with.

#	Name	Qualified	Aware of Marketplace Disruption	Problem: Customer churn	Problem: Availability of recycled materials	Problem: Price of recycled materials	Problem: Trust with suppliers	Problem: Volume available from suppliers	Follow Up?
1	Atlas Daniel	TRUE	1	2	1	1	1	1	TRUE
2	Terence Campbell	FALSE	1	2		1			FALSE
3	Alexis Kelley	TRUE	1	1	1		2	1	TRUE
4	Pippa Fenton	TRUE		1	3	1	1	1	FALSE
5	Adeel Santana	TRUE	1	1	1	1			FALSE
6	Leja Shah	TRUE		1	1		1	1	TRUE
7	Elwood Noel	TRUE	1	1	1		2	1	TRUE
8	Tiarna Everett	TRUE	1	1	1		1	1	FALSE
9	Kareena Davies	TRUE	1	1	1	1			TRUE
10	Gurleen Wilcox	TRUE	1	2	1	3			TRUE
11	Carson Foreman	TRUE	1	1	3	1	1	1	TRUE
12	Stephen Dickens	TRUE	1	1	1		1	3	TRUE
13	Mae Kerr	TRUE		1	1	1		1	FALSE
	Frequency Amongst Qualifieds:		9	14	16	9	10	11	
	Most Frequent, Important Problem! ^^^^								

The Insights Grid helps entrepreneurs to quantify their qualitative research.

The Insights Grid provided in the Startup Tactics PMR Workbook allows entrepreneurs to quantify their qualitative research. This relies on the entrepreneur's ability to notice and document the pain points that PMR participants describe. In the grid, each PMR participant gets a row and each column represents a problem or theme that emerged in at least one interview or observation session. As PMR continues, new problems or themes are added as additional columns. In each cell, a rating on a scale of 3 is included for the severity of the problem or weight of a theme for the participant. For example, a rating of 3 would be an acute problem/challenge, while 1 would be a light issue. After conducting a significant number of PMR sessions, the data from qualified participants who match the characteristics in the End User Profile are tallied to determine which problems or challenges are the most frequent and most severe for end users. The use of the Insights Grid effectively requires a careful balance between problems and themes that are too broad and those that are too narrow.

The Insights Grid lets you come back with a far more compelling statement, such as "I have spoken to X people and found that 73% of them face a problem with Y." The systematic approach to identifying the data trends through the PMR process helps to surface relevant insights for analysis.

Quantifying PMR with Surveys

After all the interviews, observation, and immersion, you probably have some pretty strong hypotheses regarding your end users, their pain points, and other factors that will contribute to how you design, build, and market your product. However, at this point those are primarily based on anecdotal evidence.

While detailed, in-depth interactions are invaluable, relying solely on this limited number of data points is a bit risky and may impact your ability to gain the confidence of your colleagues and investors. To verify that your PMR findings apply to the market at large, you can use surveys to better quantify the opportunity and gather more evidence that your assumptions and hypotheses are correct.

For example, in your interviews and observations you found a common thread that most of your target end users struggle with aggregating accurate billable hours for each client so they can be invoiced on the first of the month. Every day an invoice slips is another day of delay in receiving funds that fuel their business operations, so there are real financial implications. That's a solid pain point that your (still theoretical) product could solve with its mobile app and real-time reporting dashboard.

But there's still a chance that even though this issue was cited frequently during your interviews and observations, it's actually not that pervasive a problem in the industry at large. Here's where the survey comes in.

You can get a far broader pool of individuals who match your End User Profile to answer a few quick questions in an online form, so you should design your survey to capture the data points you need to prove—or disprove—your hypotheses. The survey might ask:

- Do your billable staff get their hours in on time?
- Is your ability to invoice impacted by a lack of timely data?
- How important is the ability to invoice and receive funds from clients ASAP?

With just a few questions, you'll now be able to say with confidence that, for instance, 80% of firms have trouble with collecting billable hours in a timely fashion, 50% say this impacts their ability to invoice, and 65% rank the ability to invoice promptly as a major or significant priority. The example illustrates that, while this pain point isn't universal, it's pervasive enough that a decent-sized target market exists that might respond to your solution's value proposition. We'll develop more significant proof of this in subsequent tactics as well.

And, of course, if those percentages were much lower across the board, it might indicate that the prospects you did deep-dive PMR with are outliers rather than representative of the typical company in this space. This information can help you adjust your offering, reset expectations, or pivot altogether.

Creating the surveys themselves isn't particularly difficult or expensive, with free options such as SurveyMonkey or Google Forms adequate for this stage of your venture's development. The hard part is coming up with the right questions—you don't want to overwhelm respondents with too many questions or "lead the witness" with question-and-answer combinations that might skew your data—and then finding and incentivizing members of your target end user population to participate.

Incorporating Additional Secondary Market Research

While it's essential for your venture to conduct extensive primary market research on its own to truly understand customer needs, secondary market research (i.e., research conducted by third parties) should also play a limited role at several key junctures.

When you're first starting out, secondary market research can provide a good sense of the overall market for your solution. It will highlight the key terminology and trends for the industry and give you a solid foundation of baseline knowledge so you don't come off as uninformed or unprofessional.

Published reports from analyst firms can be pricey but may be worth the upfront investment depending on how well you already know the space. But even if you can't afford to purchase all the ones you'd like, much of this research is also disseminated in press releases, news articles, and white papers commissioned by vendors. Just be sure to check your sources to ensure you're working with accurate and recent data.

As your venture matures and you have more financial resources at your disposal, secondary market research can also play a role when it comes to market sizing, competitive intelligence, and identifying emerging innovations and technology. If budget allows, you can leverage more comprehensive research services and databases to fuel your sales process, including for finding key decision-makers and other relevant information about prospects such as their revenues, headcounts, and organizational structures.

Next Steps

Using the insights gained through the PMR process, it is time to begin truly testing the market with the refined End User Profile that your PMR has helped you to develop. Before actively marketing and selling your solution, you will need some assets to communicate your quantified value proposition to potential customers clearly and concisely.

EXAMPLE

FindOurView

Co-founded by George Whitfield and Rita Ma and joined by Mark Pothen and Parth Agrawal, FindOurView began with a vision to drive empathy and nuance in the way communities are heard and understood in large-scale conversations, using generative AI. With a goal to build a profitable business that has potential to positively impact public discourse, they examined a range of commercial applications that could align with their raison d'être.

The team conducted primary market research interviews on hundreds of potential customers, studying needs in market segments such as journalism, government, employee engagement, and user research. At first they collected results in Google Docs and Sheets, but as they gathered more results it gradually became more time consuming to find and track new insights in comparison to their prior research.

	PMR Lead	Market Segment	Interview Time	Interview Format	Done	Key Takeaways	Interviewer 1	Interviewer 2
40	First name Last name	Employee Engagement / Growth stage	1/5/2023, 11:00 AM	Video	☑	• Used OfficeVibe for weekly surveys with 75% response rate • Responses were anonymous and shown to whole company • Reading/replying to employees is key to high response rate • Spent weeks tagging/replying to 500 when she first arrived • Prefers to use weekly surveys over 1-on-1s for remote team	Mar...	Rita ...
41	First name Last name	Gov/Resident Feedback	1/5/2023, 1:00 PM	Video	☑	• City planning managers run surveys for various initiatives • Planning data analyst supports all the planning managers • Struggling to analyze open-end text and wants a solution • Positive influencer for sales to city planning managers	Geo...	Part...
42	First name Last name	Employee Engagement / Growth stage	1/6/2023, 1:00 PM	Video	☑	• Industry in "productivity paranoia" due to economy, layoffs • After reorg/layoffs must focus on retention of key people • Runs Culture Amp quarterly surveys and likes benchmarks • Hard to get motivation data from surveys or mgr. 1-on-1s	Rita ...	Geo...
43	First name Last name	Gov/Resident Feedback	1/6/2023, 2:00 PM	Video	☑	• Watering hole: conference on deliberative democracy • Cities and districts are trying participatory budgeting • Involves collecting, sorting, discussing, picking ideas • Sorting is too slow - experimenting w/tech to speed up	Part...	Mar...

Table in coda.io listing key takeaways from each interview that was performed and linking to other tables that have additional information on the customer (PMR Lead) who was interviewed and the market segment being investigated.

To address this problem, they built a set of linked tables using coda.io, tracking their interview contacts, notes, and key takeaways. They also built tables to specify market characteristics, hypotheses, and End User Profiles. Finally, they wrote scripts that automatically pulled results of each interview into an insight grid showing the status of hypotheses they were testing in each market. This reduced the time to track and compare results, although the process of finding insights was still manual.

Hypotheses on this End User Profile

🔍 Search

☐ Description	Tests	Validated	Inalidated	Validations on this End User Profile	Invalidations on this End User Profile
Is spending a significant amount of time interviewing customers to explore new markets or design new products	8	75%	25%	Ron M on 3/29/2023, 12:00 PM Kathy J on 3/24/2023, 10:30 AM Kirk D on 2/19/2023, 10:00 AM Gary N on 2/20/2023, 12:00 PM Vivek P on 3/22/2023, 1:00 PM Mitch S on 3/7/2023, 1:00 PM	Molly T on 2/27/2023, 3:00 PM Aaron P on 3/29/2023, 12:00 PM
Is spending too much time analyzing notes and transcripts collected from customer interviews	7	29%	71%	Kathy J on 3/24/2023, 10:30 AM Rory S on 2/22/2023, 11:00 AM	Kirk D on 2/19/2023, 10:00 AM Gary N on 2/20/2023, 12:00 PM Glenn T on 2/21/2023, 5:30 PM Elizabeth T on 3/13/2023, 11:00 AM Mitch S on 3/7/2023, 1:00 PM
Needs to transfer insights about the customers to other members of the team	6	33%	67%	Kathy J on 3/24/2023, 10:30 AM Noah L on 2/19/2023, 8:00 AM	Elizabeth T on 3/13/2023, 11:00 AM Aaron P on 3/29/2023, 12:00 PM Ron M on 3/29/2023, 12:00 PM Gary N on 2/20/2023, 12:00 PM
Is spending too much time and effort preparing questions or hypotheses for customer interviews	2	50%	50%	Kathy J on 3/24/2023, 10:30 AM	Glenn T on 2/21/2023, 5:30 PM
Is having difficulty showing a repeatable sales process to justify an upcoming round of funding	2	50%	50%	Kathy J on 3/24/2023, 10:30 AM	Vivek P on 3/22/2023, 1:00 PM

Table in coda.io aggregating the status of hypotheses that were tested over the course of multiple interviews, including the total number of tests performed, the percentage of tests validated or invalidated, and the specific interviews in which the hypotheses were tested.

Through their research they discovered that many other founders felt the process of finding insights in customer interviews takes too long and that this problem persists over the life of the company. Realizing that this could be solved by FindOurView's technology, they built a product that uses AI to read interview transcripts, validate hypotheses, and make the results more accessible via a chatbot. They solved their interview efficiency problem and found an attractive market opportunity for their business in the space of customer research.

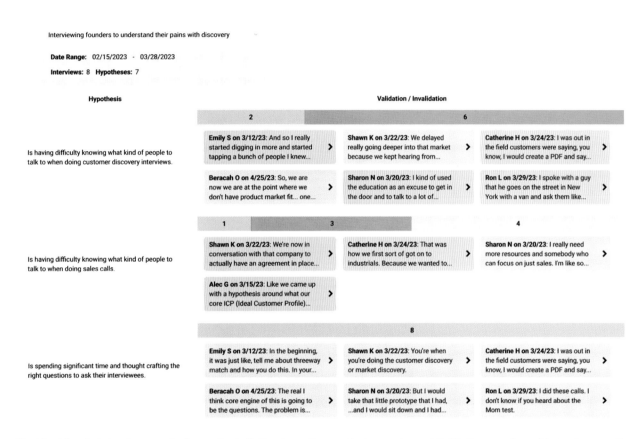

Interviewing founders to understand their pains with discovery

Date Range: 02/15/2023 - 03/28/2023

Interviews: 8 **Hypotheses:** 7

Hypothesis	Validation / Invalidation		

FindOurView's interview analysis product, listing hypotheses that were tested (left); the number of interviews validated (green bar), invalidated (red bar), or untested (gray bar); and quotes supporting each validation or invalidation that was performed.

Summary

Market research may involve a small amount of secondary market research upfront to familiarize yourself with the industry. The bulk of your market research should be in-depth primary market research that starts qualitative in nature. Your job is to get to know your end user as well as you know your best friends. This will be from a combination of interviews, observation, and immersion. The insights you gather can be quantified before launching any surveys and this will help you to communicate what you've learned to others. Gathering insights through a systematic process will help to inform how you design your go-to-market approach. You're looking for "aha" moments in which you disprove something you previously believed.

TOOLS OF THE TRADE

Note Taking

Coda (coda.io)

Notion (notion.so)

Google Docs (docs.google.com)

Watering Holes

User Interviews (userinterviews.com)

Facebook Groups (facebook.com)

LinkedIn Groups (linkedin.com)

Reddit (reddit.com)

Recording

Otter (otter.ai)

Fireflies (fireflies.ai)

Grain (grain.com)

Surveys

Google Forms (google.com/forms/about)

Qualtrics (qualtrics.com)

SurveyMonkey (surveymonkey.com)

PROMPTS

1. Immersion: Identify 3 competitors/alternatives from Step 11, Competitive Position, and sign up for their services.
2. Maintaining Relationships: Write an outreach email to interviewees you've already talked to.
3. Expanding Your PMR Pool: Find 20 people you can reach out to.
4. Making Sense of PMR Feedback: Develop your qual/quant matrix.
5. Quantifying Things Further with Surveys: Design a survey to send out.

WORKBOOK

Get the Startup Tactics PMR Workbook, which will help you expand your PMR efforts, systematize your analysis for quantitative insights, and learn more about your customers. Within you will find worksheets that include:

1. Hypotheses, Goals, and Script: You need to have a script to loosely follow in PMR.
2. Qualifications: You need to define who exactly you're looking to conduct research with.
3. Existing Subjects: You should have a list of existing interviewees to go back to.
4. Watering Holes: You should expand your pool of participants with new watering holes.
5. Outreach: You should carefully craft outreach to new and existing participants.
6. Tracking and Scheduling: You should have a tracker for each of your conversations.
7. Notes: You will need to gather your qualitative findings and notes for easy review.
8. Insights Grid: You can leverage the insights grid to quantify the insights you gather.
9. Survey Design: Once ready, you can design and run a survey to expand your data set.

ADDITIONAL RESOURCES

→ **Get the Workbook!** Visit StartupTactics.net/market-research

TACTIC 4

Assets

Developing Startup Visual Assets

Entrepreneurs can create a potentially impactful innovation, but unless your stakeholders have a comprehensive understanding of how you deliver value, your ability to generate demand or acquire resources diminishes rapidly.

After conducting a baseline amount of PMR—knowing that the process never truly ends—and quantifying insights from your qualitative research, you are prepared to begin exploring how your hypothesized product and market fit in the real world with real people. We will explore that through highly targeted marketing and sales efforts.

You'll need some visual assets to effectively communicate what you plan to provide. The key for these early-stage visual assets is developing them so they're fast, easily updated, and concise.

In This Tactic, You Will:

- Build a remarkably simple brand for your venture.
- Learn about using clear and concise visual assets such as graphics, animations, or videos to communicate the value your venture creates.
- Build out a simple website, social profiles, and content for your audience.

Building a Brand

Before you begin any marketing exercises you should have a "brand." I put the word "brand" in quotes because you do not need to have a fully fleshed-out, perfected brand at this point in time. Our goal in moving forward with marketing and sales tactics is to validate the accuracy of our PMR learnings, not necessarily to optimize them, which would require a fine-tuned brand.

At this point, you just need a preliminary brand so you present as an actual company, not just as a curious entrepreneur. A basic brand can be a color, an icon, and a wordmark. One brand I built was quite simply the name of my proposed company in a font that made sense. I started by searching for stencil fonts on DaFont.com, a website I had visited many times when younger. I typed in the name of our company and got a sense of the options available:

A search for "stencil" fonts on DaFont.com provided early potential brands.

While not flashy, it led to the early brand for our company Work Today. This brand is not where we ended up, but it provided something for the early marketing and sales tests and experiments, which led to our first paying customers.

Other tools today offer the ability to rapidly make logos, such as Canva's logo designer. With tools like these, you can create your first brand in as little as 10 minutes. That initial brand is enough to get you going.

With so much still unproven at this point, it's best to conserve resources by testing with a "good enough" brand to zero in on the right target customer. Your brand will change based on early marketing and sales experiments. At that stage, it makes more sense to invest in a full brand exercise since it will be less likely to change.

Explaining What You Do and How You Do It

One of the hardest things to do is explain what you do and how you do it when you are working on a new venture for two main reasons. First, you are introducing something new into the world that others, specifically your end users, do not yet understand, so there's a learning curve. And second, you are an unproven new venture, so it is hard to maintain someone's attention. This necessitates visual assets to effectively communicate and educate the audience on what you do and the value you provide.

Graphics are a helpful option for explaining simple concepts. Animations take it to another level by providing a short, concise, visual representation of how your proposed product creates value. Videos can also close those gaps, and many new ventures offer explainer videos. Whether graphics, animations, or videos, these visual assets are an extremely valuable and scalable way to quickly explain the new thing you are introducing to the world.

DISCIPLINED
ENTREPRENEURSHIP

REFER TO STEP

3

END USER
PROFILE

Creating these new visual assets can get expensive, however, and they will need to change as you learn from your marketing and sales experiments. But custom graphics, animations, and videos aren't as pricey as you may think. You can source designers online who can help you to create these for as little as $50. The simplest approach, however, is creating your visual assets in presentation tools like Power-Point or Google Slides, which both have animation capabilities. This DIY approach ensures you can make rapid iterations as you learn.

Website

Your brand—including the logo and the additional visual assets that you develop—should be showcased somewhere online, so you'll need to create a basic website. At the earliest stages, you should be able to create the website yourself, starting with just one page. There is no sense in overinvesting or overexplaining your venture online at this point, and a simple page accomplishes more than you'd think. Much of the content and language on your website will change, so begin by simply adding the information you already have from your business plan to save some time.

To simplify the process and quickly iterate as you learn from your experiments, start with a template from a website hosting platform, such as Squarespace, Wix, or WordPress. You will also need the capability to create additional individual landing pages to support the marketing experiments that you will run. You might also leverage tools such as Unbounce and Strikingly for the rapid creation of simple landing pages before you have extensive information that you already know resonates with your target customers. These two tools, and others like them, will allow you to quickly put a value proposition in front of a potential customer.

Social Profiles

To complement your website, you should also have social profiles set up to present your new venture to the world. When you begin running your marketing experiments, many will be tied to your social profiles. It's also possible when you run your sales experiments that prospects you reach out to will look you up online to understand your business in more detail.

Unlike your website, however, social media isn't a set-it-and-forget-it affair. You'll need to regularly generate new posts and content; otherwise, these accounts won't appear as active, going concerns. In fact, a little-used account may come across as abandoned or make potential customers question the legitimacy and viability of your product or company. Be prepared to post consistently on any social media account you create.

With this in mind, new ventures should be selective about which platforms to invest their time into. For starters, any platform where you're planning to advertise must have a corresponding social media account for your brand. That way when prospects engage with your ads, they can view your account for more context and follow you even if they're not ready to make a purchase at the moment.

Beyond that, your selection of social media platforms should be driven by which ones are most actively used by your target market for purposes related to your product. This last bit is essential because, for example, many potential users of your online accounting software might have Instagram accounts, but they're probably not using those when making purchasing decisions about things for work.

A LinkedIn account for your company is table stakes regardless of your target market, because investors, partners, and potential future hires will all begin there when researching you.

And for a B2B offering, LinkedIn might be home to the majority of your social media activity. Posts should be text heavy unless you can leverage infographics or other data-driven imagery.

Twitter—now X—used to be another crucial platform for B2B products to engage on with short, quippy teasers, but that platform's future is in some doubt based on its new ownership and management and looming replacements waiting in the winds. However, a quick search of hashtags relevant to your product and perusing your competitors' activity can give you a sense of how active things are now for your space.

Consumer-oriented brands have a lot more social platforms to choose from, and good content often comes with higher production values. Instagram and TikTok posts are highly visual and often incorporate video or voice-overs. Pinterest might make sense for extremely visual products with a refined design aesthetic, such as furniture or home decor.

Facebook is the old guard in social media and may not be as "cool" as it used to be, but it's still a popular spot for adults to share updates with friends and family and connect with brands. But if your post doesn't have strong visuals, don't even bother.

Facebook Groups, however, are a whole different animal and are used just as much for professional purposes as for more frivolous affinity purposes. If there are Facebook Groups related to your product's space, engaging in those forums might pay off by getting in front of some potential early adopters.

Social media also isn't just about you and your product. While you can certainly broadcast messages, the intent of these platforms is to be interactive and engage with the broader community. That means actively following other social media accounts, including "liking" and/or commenting when relevant.

These activities aren't just window dressing, however. Your company's social media presence and thought leadership extends to the conversations you engage in online and which posts you share on your own account. The more you contribute in forums where your target Personas are present, the more opportunities to build awareness and a positive reputation.

That said, you don't want to spend all your time managing your social media profiles, so narrow your focus to topics and conversations where your company's expertise or your product's value proposition is truly relevant and likely to burnish your brand's reputation.

Content Generation

Aside from the solution's basics, you might want to add additional visual and/or text-based content on your website, including videos, blog posts, and articles. Using search engine optimization (SEO), this content will improve your site's online discoverability, plus you can point people from your marketing and sales experiments to relevant online resources.

Begin by identifying what your end users are seeking online, tapping both your PMR and online SEO tools to define trends and keywords. This can serve as the foundation for your early content strategy, whether you're creating it yourself, outsourcing to designers and writers, or using generative artificial intelligence tools. There are a variety of approaches you could take to generate content for your business, including hiring a designer to draft the content, drafting the content in-house using traditional tools, and even drafting the content using generative artificial intelligence (GenAI) tools.

Leveraging Generative AI

Some example scenarios where you could consider using GenAI include:

- Logo design
- Marketing text and images for your website
- Graphic design of a landing page
- New descriptions and perspectives on your Persona
- Images and script for your explainer video
- Ad campaign text and images

Today there are many GenAI tools available online that can assist you in generating content in a variety of formats, including text (ChatGPT, Bard), images (Midjourney, Stable Diffusion), and video (Runway). These tools generally use large language models (LLMs) that are trained on a wide variety of data sources, enabling them to produce content that often rivals the quality of what a human might create. However, these models lack specific insights into your business. To get them to produce content that you can use, you must write a prompt that gives clear instructions on the result you wish to receive. The usefulness of the result will depend heavily on the content that you provide in your prompt.

The optimal structure of your prompt will depend on the specific tool you are using to generate the content. Before you begin using a GenAI tool, you should search online for guidelines on prompt engineering in the context of the tool you are using. For example, in the case of ChatGPT, your prompt might include one or more paragraphs of text describing your desired result, background context, and instructions on the approach to take in crafting the response. You might ask it to follow a step-by-step approach in crafting its response (also known as chain-of-thought prompting), or you could ask it to critique the response it provides, to improve the quality. Since these tools are rapidly advancing, when getting started it is always a good idea to search for the latest best practices and examples of high-quality prompt engineering.

Materials you could use in your prompt:

- Quantified value proposition
- High-level product specification
- One-pager, brief, or executive summary
- SEO keywords you found in other tools
- Existing marketing, ad copy
- Existing images and graphic designs
- Careful description of your goal for the content

What not to use:

- Anything proprietary
- Your secret sauce
- Intellectual property

While GenAI can accelerate your path to drafting content, there are some caveats to consider. For example, according to a ruling in US Federal Court on August 18, 2023,[1] you cannot copyright artwork that is produced using GenAI. This may impact the type of content you wish to produce using GenAI tools, and you should think about what digital assets your business needs to own versus what might be acceptable not to own in deciding what to produce using GenAI. For example, you will likely want to own your logo and brand imagery as you grow your business into a more recognizable presence. However, you might not need to own certain advertising copy that you are producing, especially if you are using it in a quick, iterative test.

In addition, GenAI models can hallucinate, meaning they will sometimes produce content that is either factually inaccurate or contextually inappropriate to your work. As such, it's important to carefully review content that is produced before incorporating it into your business processes.

---

[1] https://news.bloomberglaw.com/ip-law/ai-generated-art-lacks-copyright-protection-d-c-court-rules

EXAMPLES

Invictus BCI

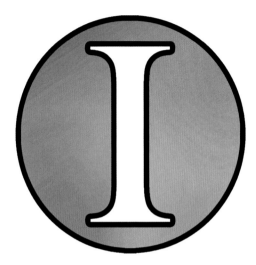

Focused on improving the lives of amputees everywhere, Vini and Eeshan Tripathii, MIT Electrical Engineering and Computer Science '23, set out to commercialize brain control interfaces. Their first product was designed for upper-arm amputees, inspired by the experience of someone close to the siblings who had lost a hand. After thorough market segmentation, they found that there are plenty of prosthetics on the market and—while extremely expensive—the true problem was that current models were difficult to control. Their PMR revealed that amputees are so dissatisfied with these systems that 60% give up on using their prosthetics—they would rather use nothing at all.

Their solution supported individual digit control. It is as intuitive to use as the human hand and robust enough to handle external conditions such as sweat. Activities that were near impossible before—like typing, driving, cooking, buttoning a shirt, and cutting with scissors—become possible. Confronting a variety of challenges—including refining their end-user profile, ensuring they had a large enough *beachhead* Total Addressable Market (TAM), working through complex technical issues, and exploring regulatory approval—they faced an issue even simpler. What is their solution?

The high-level product specification required a more visual explanation. Their board members in the MIT delta v program had incorrect impressions even after having spent hours with the team. The challenge was that the technology being developed was incredibly complex—leveraging EMG and EEG sensors—and the board remained unclear on what the product was exactly. Some thought it was the prosthetic, while others thought it was the behind-the-scenes software technology.

The pair of entrepreneurs were developing a headset sensor for the brain and a sleeve to transmit the data to the prosthetic. They struggled with communicating this until they introduced a simple animation to demonstrate the product. In the animation, the headset lowered onto the end user's head and the sleeve slid onto the end user's arm before the prosthetic was added. This simple, short animation provided clarity about what the product was in a matter of seconds.

➔ **See it live!** Check out the full animation: StartupTactics.net/startup-assets/invictusbci

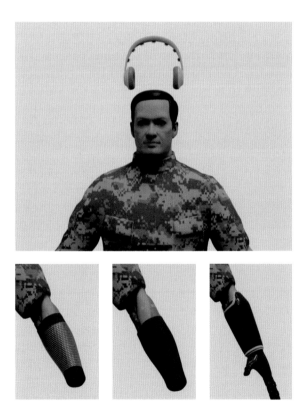

Screenshots from an animation demonstrating the functionality provided by Invictus BCI's technology. Here the headset and sleeve are highlighted.

Memorable AI

 memorable

You might recall Camilo Fosco and his company Memorable AI from the introduction. Fosco developed complex artificial intelligence technology to help advertisers optimize visuals and campaigns before running them. The technology analyzes advertisements and identifies a large variety of key components such as logo position, semantic elements, human poses, dominant colors, and more. It then predicts how the ad will perform across several marketing KPIs, including click-through-rate and brand lift, but also cognitive dimensions that are typically hard to estimate like recall (whether a viewer will remember the ad) and attention (whether the ad will be looked at, and what parts of it are more eye-catching). It finally recommends changes and can even redesign the advertisement.

The value proposition for such complex technology is difficult to explain, especially in such a short period of time. Knowing they had a matter of seconds to explain their technology to potential customers, Fosco and the team developed a brief outlining the components of a potential animation that would allow anyone to rapidly comprehend the value of their technology. This animation demonstrated the solution's capabilities and improved the conversion rate of getting homepage visitors to book product demos.

The new animated assets, alongside a redesign of their webpage, netted them a 123% increase on Book-A-Demo clicks over a two-week period after deployment.

ADDITIONAL RESOURCES

→ **See it live!** Check out the full animation: StartupTactics.net/startup-assets/memorableai

memorable

Products ▾   Why Memorable   Case Studies   Blog   Careers   Partners   Request Access

High-accuracy AI to improve branding and the performance of every ad

Test & optimize your assets in seconds with deep learning and cognitive science models built with millions of human reactions

Join Memorable

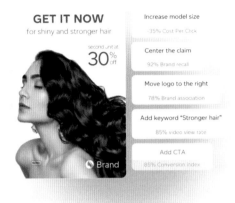

Screenshots from an animation demonstrating how Memorable AI's artificial intelligence technology can analyze an existing advertisement, identify weaknesses in the design, make recommendations, and redesign the advertisement.

Summary

As you prepare to go to market, you will need to appear as an established business. This requires some of the visual assets that all other businesses have. You can take an expedited approach to building a logo, website, and social profiles for the sole purpose of getting them live. They will all change. On a related note, you have a new venture that is preparing to launch a solution that is not yet known to the world. Given the complexity of your new proposed solution, you need to communicate it clearly. The problem is that complex solutions usually need time to communicate and you will lose your audience's attention before they understand what you provide. Building visual assets or animations can help to communicate your value in a matter of seconds.

TOOLS OF THE TRADE

Brand and Logos

Canva (canva.com)

99designs (99designs.com)

DesignCrowd (designcrowd.com)

Fiverr (fiverr.com)

Domain Name

GoDaddy (godaddy.com)

Namecheap (namecheap.com)

Ionos (ionos.com)

Websites

Squarespace (squarespace.com)

Wix (wix.com)

WordPress (wordpress.com)

Unbounce (unbounce.com)

Strikingly (strikingly.com)

Social Profiles

Facebook (facebook.com)

Instagram (instagram.com)

LinkedIn (linkedin.com)

TikTok (tiktok.com)

Snapchat (snapchat.com)

Newsletter

Mailchimp (mailchimp.com)

ConstantContact (constantcontact.com)

HubSpot (hubspot.com)

Content Generation

Upwork (upwork.com)

Fiverr (fiverr.com)

ChatGPT (chat.openai.com)

Midjourney (midjourney.com)

Bard (bard.google.com)

Stable Diffusion (stability.ai/stablediffusion)

Synthesia (synthesia.io)

Memorable.ai Ad Maker (admaker.memorable.io)

AdCreative.ai (adcreative.ai)

Predis.ai (predis.ai)

Invideo.ai (invideo.io)

Runway (research.runwayml.com)

PROMPTS

1. Design your logo or write a brief of what you want and source a designer.
2. Set up a website and begin laying out the content that you will need.
3. Create a landing page with a specific value prop/call to action.
4. Conduct keyword research to determine content that will attract your Persona.
5. Write the script for an explainer video and find a vendor to create it for you.
6. Or, create your explainer video using an online explainer video generation tool.
7. Write a brief for an animation or graphic that you can use and source a designer or animator to create it for you.
8. Evaluate sources to find a contractor online and post/share your briefs.

WORKBOOK

Get the Startup Tactics Assets Workbook, which will help you build your brand, create visual assets, and develop a customer-facing website. Within you will find worksheets that include:

1. Logo: Determine what your early logo should look like.
2. Visual Medium: Determine the best-fit type of visual for communicating your value.
3. Creative Brief: Write up a brief for a freelancer to create a graphic, animation, or video.
4. Tools and Resources: Identify online freelancers/resources to outsource visual creation.
5. Domains: Get creative and identify available domain names for your business.
6. Website Content: Determine the types and amount of content for your initial website.
7. Website Platforms: Identify a variety of options to build and host your new website.
8. Social Profiles: Determine which social profiles you need and get them created.
9. Email and Signature: Set up your new email with a compelling, official signature.

ADDITIONAL RESOURCES

➜ **Get the Workbook!** Visit StartupTactics.net/startup-assets

Marketing

Proving Persona Assumptions with Digital Advertising

With your insights from PMR and some visual assets to put in front of people, it's time to test things out in the real world! We will explore both marketing and sales, which will be the key components of your early go-to-market strategy. The goals for the early marketing and sales tactics are:

1. Testing and refining your proposed End User Profile, Quantified Value Proposition, and high-level product specification
2. Gathering data that helps with future decision-making as your business evolves
3. Building a list of the people who will be your first customers

While exploring the marketing and sales tactics, it is important for B2B companies to remember that you are building a list of *people* who will be your first customers, *not businesses*. Businesses do not buy things; people who happen to work for businesses buy things.

The marketing and sales tactics add prospects to the top of your funnel. You cannot have a bottom of the funnel without filling the top first. Through these two tactics, you should be able to build repeatable go-to-market motions.

In This Tactic, You Will:

- Build a mousetrap to rapidly test value propositions with your target end users out in the real-world.

- Identify the most appropriate advertising platform, set a budget, and plan a digital advertising campaign targeting end users with your value proposition.

- Develop an understanding of the metrics that matter when running early advertising experiments.

- Turn those who responded to your ads into a list of individuals who are interested in your Quantified Value Proposition—who might be your first customers!

Overall Marketing Strategy

Your business will employ a variety of marketing approaches over the course of time and will require a comprehensive well-rounded marketing strategy. This tactic looks specifically at how you can leverage online advertising at the earliest stages. Why? Because online advertising platforms provide you with the most control regarding input data, such as who you would like to target and when, compared to other means of marketing when you do not yet have customers or are looking to experiment with new customer segments. Not to mention that online advertising is also relatively inexpensive and allows you to run micro-experiments with small ad buys.

DISCIPLINED
ENTREPRENEURSHIP

REFER TO STEP

2

BEACHHEAD
MARKET

REFER TO STEP

19

COST OF
CUSTOMER
ACQUISITION

Because you can set very specific parameters for who will see your online advertisement, you have more control using these platforms than with any other medium. Unlike a billboard—where a broad audience sees the advertisement and the only targeting parameter is location—online advertising gives you control over exactly who will see your ad. This control saves you money by reaching only those people in your Beachhead Market and saves time by generating leads only from that limited pool of prospects.

Online advertising also provides you with data on current and previous campaigns to inform future decisions, including further refining your messaging and visuals. Finally, online advertising provides you with the ability to make rapid changes and run quick experiments to test new hypotheses.

While extremely helpful for an early-stage startup or a business looking to expand with new products or market segments, in the long term you'll need a holistic marketing strategy to optimize the cost of customer acquisition. And online advertising may not be the best for you; that's up to you to decide. Your business is unique, so while you may choose to employ a different advertising medium initially, remember that you need the same level of control to target exclusively those in your Beachhead Market. Keep in mind also that while you might be focused on direct, outbound sales to get your first customers, every business needs some marketing as well to bring in new leads and build a scalable, repeatable sales process.

Mousetrap Model

"Mousetraps" are a way to determine whether your prospective end users are enticed by your value proposition before ever building the product. You provide the "bait" (i.e., messaging and imagery around your Quantified Value Proposition) and see whether people take the bait and get ensnared in the trap, which in this case is simply adding their name and email to a waiting list, subscribing to a newsletter, registering for a live demo, or even preordering. Much like you might try out different foods for bait to catch a pesky mouse (a little cheese one day, some peanut butter the next), your mousetraps can test how your value proposition and messaging perform as bait for potential customers.

Luckily, building these landing page mousetraps is quite easy and cheap. You really don't want much at all on these pages; the more that's on there, the less certainty you'll have regarding which element turned prospects off or compelled them to sign up for your mailing list.

These landing pages usually just need one image that evokes the Persona, the problem, or the solution to draw in the target audience, along with a headline and just a few lines of text. Resist the temptations to get creative with catchy taglines or spout off a laundry list of features and functionality, particularly if you haven't built any of them yet.

Once you've built a mousetrap, setting it involves running an ad on a digital advertising platform targeting your ideal user or buyer Persona. The advertisement should have the same or similar visuals and messaging as the mousetrap with a link to the landing page.

After the ad is run, you can determine end user interest based on the number of click-throughs from the ad and, subsequently, how many provided their information via the landing page form. This data offers an indication as to whether the target end user actually desires the Quantified Value Proposition.

Because it's such an easy lift to create these mousetrap landing pages, it might make sense to create multiple versions of your landing pages and ads that tweak the messaging with different potential Quantified Value Propositions to optimize your ultimate go-to-market approach. Emphasizing different parts of the value proposition, using different phrasing and terminology, or even just rearranging the order of selling points on the page enables you to compare results between multiple mousetraps to identify which particular combination of messaging and end user targeting works best. Now when you start committing larger dollars to lead generation, the team will have more confidence that the venture is putting its best foot forward.

Goals of Early-Stage Digital Advertising

Online advertising offers a massive range of options, from large-scale, broadly targeted consumer campaigns to micro-targeted small ad buys to reach a small but specific audience. At this stage you just need a simple process to get your first customers in the door. With a small investment, entrepreneurs can narrow their focus on to a precise set of target customers using demographics, psychographics, and watering holes.

As you dabble in early-stage digital advertising, you need clearly defined goals that relate back to the organization-level goals you set in the first tactic. For example, you might have goals related to identifying 100 potential end users in your Beachhead Market, and your early advertising activity can help you reach that goal.

However, you can also use this as an opportunity to validate the End User Profile or Quantified Value Proposition. For instance, you can test out the same value proposition with three different target audiences, or slight variations of your End User Profile, to determine—with real people—who the ideal end user truly is. You might also run an experiment with your refined target audience that presents three different Quantified Value Propositions, using the results to identify the best-fit value proposition for this crowd.

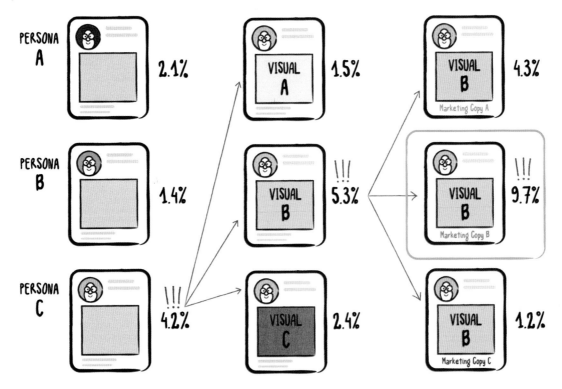

This isn't, however, the time to expend resources on building highly optimized advertising campaigns. It's too early in your journey and far too many unknowns remain. For now, focus on building advertising campaigns that teach you the most about your end user, decision-making unit, Quantified Value Proposition, and high-level product specification. This approach provides even the most confident entrepreneur with hard data that confirms that there are, in fact, end users who want your product and that it's worthwhile to actually invest resources in building it.

In time, as you narrow in on your ideal end user, you may begin to broaden your targeting slowly. As you conquer your Beachhead Market and begin expanding to follow-on markets, you will continue to adjust your experiments. If your next follow-on market focuses on providing the same product to a new market segment, then

DISCIPLINED
ENTREPRENEURSHIP

REFER TO STEP

3

END USER
PROFILE

REFER TO STEP

7

HIGH-LEVEL
PRODUCT SPECS

you will adjust the targeting. On the other hand, if your next follow-on market is providing a new product to the same market segment, you may choose to change the ad copy to reflect the new product's Quantified Value Proposition. Proceed slowly, finding focus before you begin marketing to the masses; remember that every ad click costs you your limited, valuable money.

REFER TO STEP

8

QUANTIFIED
VALUE PROP

How to Approach Digital Advertising

To dive into digital advertising, you will need to first identify the most appropriate platform to reach your target audience, build a campaign plan, and set a reasonable budget aimed at maximizing your learnings.

REFER TO STEP

14

TAM FOR FOLLOW
ON MARKETS

Platforms

Before running any advertising campaigns, carefully select an advertising platform that makes the most sense for your business at this juncture. There are thousands of advertising platforms and each works for varying use cases and different audiences. Making the wrong choice on a platform could lead to failed experiments and squandered resources, so choose carefully to improve the odds that your advertisements are successful. This selection is similar to what we explored in Tactic 4, Developing Startup Visual Assets, but our focus here is on the capability for targeting through the social media company's advertising platform rather than just the profiles you can create.

REFER TO STEP

19

COST OF
CUSTOMER
ACQUISITION

For example, B2C businesses looking to target people based on psychographics, Facebook, Instagram, and TikTok are excellent channels. These social networking and social media websites also offer advertising platforms to businesses like yours. Their in-house advertising platforms leverage vast amounts of information about what people view on their sites and across the internet, ensuring that your advertisement reaches the right individuals with extremely detailed targeting.

It is important to note that this tactic is not just relevant to B2C businesses. B2B businesses can leverage this approach to build the top of their sales funnel as well. B2B businesses might look to LinkedIn to target end users or others in your decision-making unit based on their job titles and seniority. It may be more expensive, but this reflects the fact that your cost of customer acquisition in a B2B setting will likely be higher.

Planning

You will need a predefined action plan for your ad tests. It should contain what you wish to test, in which order, and the next steps following what may be a successful or unsuccessful test. You might choose to spend the first week of experimentation aligning on the right target end user, and then use that resulting data to spend the second week trying things out to identify the best-fit Quantified Value Proposition. Further ad tests might refine the most appealing visuals or descriptions.

Budgeting

Rather than commit a large advertising budget to these experiments, you can start with as little as $10. Online advertising provides the opportunity to learn a lot with a very small investment. Depending on the platform and your target audience, you might need to spend significantly more, but you can always start small and add additional budget later.

You might choose to run your first experiment over five days with a budget of $100. This is a great starting point and you can watch the results over the course of the first 15 minutes, first hour, first day, first week, and so on to reevaluate. After reviewing the resulting metrics from the campaign, you might decide you have statistically significant results and you can confidently end the initial campaign to launch a new ad experiment. Each subsequent experiment will help you to tweak your Quantified Value Proposition, targeting of your End User Profile, targeting of others in your decision-making unit, or your ad creative including messaging and visuals.

It is likely your initial ad tests will be inefficient from a financial perspective. While you want to eventually make them as financially efficient as possible, right now it's about gathering data about your end users, which is priceless.

Digital Advertising Metrics

Your advertising and the resulting data map to your overall go-to-market funnel. Your funnel starts with ad impressions, then click-throughs, and then conversions to leads when visitors submit their contact information on the landing page.

Based on the success rate of individuals progressing through the funnel, you can determine which advertisement or Quantified Value Proposition combination resonates most with the target audience.

You will benefit most from analyzing the relative metrics rather than the absolute metrics. For example, the number of impressions is less important than the click-through rate, which indicates the percentage of individuals who saw the ad and clicked on it.

While you can find benchmarks online for the average metrics you can shoot for, I recommend focusing more on beating your own benchmarks. As a new startup, it is hard for you to compare your work to that of established organizations. For that reason, always experiment with the goal of beating the last benchmark you set.

When Nothing Works

Digital advertising helps collect data to prove that the end user is in fact interested. But in many cases, the result might be that nobody is interested at all. How do we proceed when we find that our end user does not want our Quantified Value Proposition? There are a number of next steps you can take:

1. Reevaluate your target audience: You may need to refer back to your PMR to determine whether the audience you are targeting with your advertisement accurately reflects the individuals you interviewed, observed, and believe are interested.

2. Revisit your End User Profile: You may need to shift a bit and conduct additional PMR.

3. Experiment with different value propositions: You may need to try additional experiments with different value propositions to find one that resonates with the target audience.

4. Redesign your ads: Experiment with different visuals and strong calls to action. We're programmed to tune out ads by default, so you need something really compelling to get their attention.

If none of the above actions yield better results, it might be time to pause, pivot, or simply step away from your venture. The good news is that while this is highly disappointing, you saved a significant amount of time and hadn't yet overinvested in building a product that nobody wants.

Tips and Tricks

As you move forward with online advertising, there are a few tips and tricks to keep in mind:

- **Don't create a lot of new content.** You can easily reuse elements of your business plan—such as the Quantified Value Proposition—word for word. Instead of working on flashy headlines, opt to make use of what you already created.

- **Make use of high-quality images.** Your target audience will notice the visuals before they read the words in your advertisement. Use high-quality, royalty-free stock images available online.

- **Test one thing at a time.** Don't try testing all of your hypotheses at once because you will find that it is difficult to determine what specifically causes your target audience to do, or not do, something you hope they will. Limit your experiments to one variable at a time when possible.

- **Test willingness to pay.** Use your pricing framework and leverage online ads to present different price points to your audience to gauge their willingness to pay.

- **Need some inspiration?** Check out Google's Ads Transparency Center (adstransparency.google.com). You can look up advertisements run by other companies in your industry.

DISCIPLINED
ENTREPRENEURSHIP

REFER TO STEP

16

PRICING
FRAMEWORK

Beyond Digital Advertising: Other Means of Marketing

While online advertising may have the best ROI early in your venture's development because it has such a low financial barrier to entry, your venture may need to use other methods to reach and convert members of your target audience. These supplemental activities should be used sparingly when you're still on a shoestring budget and carefully measured and evaluated for their effectiveness before committing follow-on funds.

If you're wondering why you should spend resources beyond ads, think about how often you yourself skip past, ignore, or don't engage with advertising while browsing the web or scrolling through social media apps. For any one ad that grabs our attention, we barely notice dozens of other ones. Therefore, we must use other approaches to expand our reach.

Media coverage is just about the best free advertising you can find, so research which publications, websites, reporters, bloggers, YouTubers, podcasters, and influencers cover the industry or consumer segment you're targeting. Send them press releases and offer one-on-one product demos to get on their radar (customer stories and stats always help). You can also try local news publications and TV stations and work the "local business" angle for some additional coverage.

You can also nab some influential early adopters by submitting your solution to Product Hunt.

In-person events may be analog, but they can be another effective way to publicize your offering. Pick niche events that really cater to your target audience rather than "big tent" affairs like the Consumer Electronics Show where you're unlikely to stand out. If it's a good fit, you might consider a small booth, sponsoring an event (or some swag in the conference goody bags), or applying to be a presenter. Remember that your presentation should be interesting thought leadership and offer value to attendees and not just be a blatant ad for your product; co-presenting with a bigger brand or a satisfied customer increases your chances of being selected. If those don't pan out or they exceed your budget, even just attending the conference and doing a lot of schmoozing may yield some good connections and leads. Don't be afraid to try smaller venues, such as local user groups, professional associations, and chambers of commerce. While not super scalable, it can help you refine your pitch and build out your pipeline.

EXAMPLE

Livvi

Madeleine Cooney, MIT Sloan MBA '23, and Anisha Quadir, MIT Sloan MBA and Harvard Kennedy School MPP '23, had lived the experience of moving to a new city and shared the frustrating process of making new friends. They founded their business, Livvi (formerly known as Bloom), to help others by providing a unique mobile application to help build and sustain female friendships.

With a proposed End User Persona—Katie—and a hypothesized value proposition, Cooney and Quadir leveraged online advertising to build their waitlist. They developed ads to target users online matching their End User Profile:

- Young women originally from the Midwest who just graduated from small colleges
- Moved to a city in the Northeast for work

- Employed in entry-level marketing roles
- Making $40k–$50k per year

These users saw the ads presenting Livvi's Quantified Value Proposition and upon clicking were taken to a simple landing page, where they were prompted to provide their email address to join the Livvi waitlist.

As the founding duo experimented with their ad tests, they wanted to see which primary visual was the most appealing to the demographic. They chose a set of images that evoke slightly different spirits and offerings behind their brand. They created three different landing pages that contained the exact same copy and information, but different background images. They used A/B testing, or split testing, using the Leadpages platform to run the test. These specifications ensured that the test was being run in a controlled manner. In addition to running paid ads, they also posted about the company in relevant Facebook groups that were focused on friend-finding to increase exposure. The Leadpages platform randomized the images that each visitor saw.

	Picture	Description	Unique Visitors	Sign Ups	Conversion Rate
	(beach image)	The first picture is of a group of women at the beach. They are outdoors, active and there is no alcohol pictured.	315	142	45%
	(picnic image)	The second picture is of a group of women at a picnic during the day. They are drinking alcohol.	308	125	41%
	(party image)	The third picture is a group of women partying. It is a darker picture that could be at a bar or nightclub.	314	108	34%

The Livvi team ran an initial experiment that showcased three different advertisements with different images. The images displayed different experiences and provided data on what resonated most with the end users.

With the new data indicating that their end users responded most strongly to the image of the beach, with individuals who are active and outdoors without alcohol, Quadir and Cooney ran another test. This time, they were interested in understanding which tagline resonated best with their audience. They designed three new ads using the most popular visual from the first ad test. The ads used different copy and the A/B testing functionality in the Meta Ads Manager ensured that the split test was run in a controlled manner across Facebook and Instagram. This second test was run with a budget of $200 over 10 days.

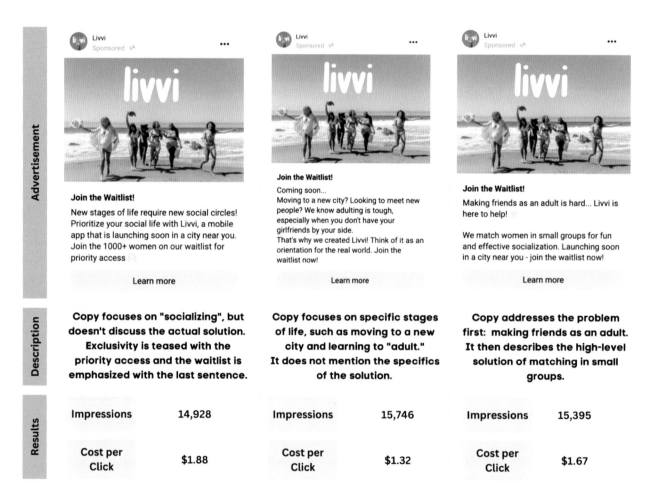

Advertisement	Join the Waitlist! New stages of life require new social circles! Prioritize your social life with Livvi, a mobile app that is launching soon in a city near you. Join the 1000+ women on our waitlist for priority access	Join the Waitlist! Coming soon... Moving to a new city? Looking to meet new people? We know adulting is tough, especially when you don't have your girlfriends by your side. That's why we created Livvi! Think of it as an orientation for the real world. Join the waitlist now!	Join the Waitlist! Making friends as an adult is hard... Livvi is here to help! We match women in small groups for fun and effective socialization. Launching soon in a city near you - join the waitlist now!
Description	Copy focuses on "socializing", but doesn't discuss the actual solution. Exclusivity is teased with the priority access and the waitlist is emphasized with the last sentence.	Copy focuses on specific stages of life, such as moving to a new city and learning to "adult." It does not mention the specifics of the solution.	Copy addresses the problem first: making friends as an adult. It then describes the high-level solution of matching in small groups.
Results	Impressions 14,928 Cost per Click $1.88	Impressions 15,746 Cost per Click $1.32	Impressions 15,395 Cost per Click $1.67

Using the highest-performing visual from the first experiment, the Livvi team ran a subsequent experiment with three different descriptions. Again, they analyzed the results to identify what resonates best with their end users.

The market testing did not end there. They continued to refine the ad copy to gather additional information:

Livvi Ad Copy - Further Testing & Optimization	Ad Impressions (# times viewed)	Ad Reach (# of unique accounts viewed)	# Results (Link Clicks)	Total Amount spent (USD)	Cost per Result (CPC)	CPM (cost per 1,000 impressions)
New to the city? Livvi is here to help you make new friends in small groups!	9,995	8,214	173	$115.58	$0.65	$11.48
Livvi helps women make friends to tackle adulthood with - because the real world needs an orientation!	8,047	7,829	108	$80.44	$0.74	$7.23
Livvi helps women prioritize their social life and make friends by matching in small groups	4,373	3,682	17	$17.55	$1.03	$4.59
There is no better time than the present to make new friends! Join Livvi today	4,598	3,798	24	$35.11	$1.30	$7.52
It's time to start prioritizing your social life again! Sign up now for priority access to Livvi.	1,383	1,305	6	$10.66	$1.45	$7.86
Making friends as an adult is hard...livvi is here to help!	1,515	1,396	5	$11.68	$2.01	$7.68

The team continued experimenting, this time with six different ad descriptions, which provided additional data on what their end users want most.

The team continued running experiments looking at more narrow targeting with ads comparing response rates in different geographic locations such as large cities versus mid-tier cities based on population and different advertisement formats. Each of these experiments led to new learnings about their ideal end user.

The waitlist grew quickly after a few experiments, indicating they had found a customer segment that connected with their Quantified Value Proposition. Over time they increased the size of their waitlist to 1,500 women. This data helped them build conviction in their customer and business plan, allowing them to move forward with the venture development process knowing that once the product was built, they had their first users ready.

Summary

You will need a comprehensive marketing strategy for your business, and in the short-term as you build your initial go-to-market you should employ low-cost, rapid experiments. The goal for these experiments should be to test whether your end users want your value proposition so that you can move forward with evidence. Further experiments can help to evaluate whether other Quantified Value Propositions are stronger or whether other customer segments are better fits. An in-depth look at online advertising presents a low-barrier approach to getting your value proposition in front of exclusively your end users, but is not usually the sole marketing required to scale the business.

TOOLS OF THE TRADE

Advertising Platforms

Meta: Facebook and Instagram (facebook.com/business/tools/ads-manager)

LinkedIn (business.linkedin.com/marketing-solutions/ads)

TikTok (ads.tiktok.com)

Snapchat (forbusiness.snapchat.com/advertising)

YouTube (youtube.com/intl/en_us/ads)

Spotify (ads.spotify.com)

Landing Page Tools

Strikingly (strikingly.com)

Wix (wix.com)

Leadpages (leadpages.com)

Unbounce (unbounce.com)

Instapage (instapage.com)

PROMPTS

1. Determine which ad platform would be the best fit for you to get started.
2. Sign up for an advertiser account on one ad platform.
3. Build a four-week plan for what you want to test.
4. Source graphics and high-quality images for your ad tests.
5. Design a set of ads where only one variable changes.
6. Develop landing pages for each ad you've built.
7. Implement visitor tracking on your landing pages.
8. Set up your ad campaign on the platform to target your Persona based on your End User Profile.

WORKBOOK

Get the Startup Tactics Marketing Workbook, which will help you design small, affordable, insightful marketing experiments to build the top of your funnel. Within you will find worksheets that include:

1. Ad Goals: Determine why you're running ads so early in your venture development.
2. Platforms: Identify the best-fit platform to reach your potential end users.
3. Experiments: Design the experiments you're setting out to test with online advertising.
4. Budget: Set a reasonable budget and max spend for your initial ad tests.
5. Findings: Pick out key insights and KPIs for each of the ads in your experiments.
6. COCA: Based on the data from your experiments calculate a reasonable COCA.
7. LTV: Estimate your customer lifetime value if you haven't already.
8. LTV:COCA: Estimate business viability with bear, base, and bull cases for LTV:COCA.

ADDITIONAL RESOURCES

→ **Get the Workbook!** Visit StartupTactics.net/marketing

Sales

Early Customer Demand Generation

06 | SALES

Entrepreneurs need a systematic approach to outbound sales outreach. It begins by targeting their ideal Persona exclusively and with precision. This tactic explores how to visualize your sales pipeline in a way that allows you to track progress toward your sales goals, build a highly targeted lead list, and construct an outreach strategy to source early customers. Entrepreneurs can explore tools to assist with sales automation making this process simpler, which has been made possible by emerging technology.

In This Tactic, You Will:

- Build your pipeline and use it to estimate value of each lead and prospect.
- Build a lead list of companies and/or individuals who are potential customers for your venture.
- Craft a sequence of compelling outreach messages to send to those on your lead list.
- Reach out to potential customers!
- Evaluate outreach to potential customers using standard metrics and revise based on the results.

"What Does Your Pipeline Look Like?"

I was once asked, "What does your pipeline look like?" At that moment, I realized I did not have a full appreciation of the way marketing and a sales pipeline contribute to the development of a business. As the CEO and/or founder, it is your job to manage pipelines.

In addition to customer pipelines, however, you must also manage the pipelines for product development, recruiting talent, fundraising, and more. As an early-stage founder, you must always have a sense of what your pipeline looks like with metrics and specific examples—beyond just your first 10 customers—because this is what will determine whether or not you hit your sales goals.

DISCIPLINED
ENTREPRENEURSHIP

REFER TO STEP

9

FIRST 10
CUSTOMERS

Marketing and Sales Stages

Refer back to your planned sales process, or decision-making process, to understand the stages of your marketing and sales pipeline. These should be mapped out and you should understand from your sales process which stages reflect marketing activities and which reflect sales activities. Some examples include leads, prospects, first product demo, follow-up sales conversation, letters of intent (LOI) and memorandums of understanding (MOU) sent, contract sent, contract signed, onboarded, and so on. At any given moment you should know which customers and potential customers are in each stage of your pipeline.

Estimated Value

While your pipeline makes it much easier to manage the sales process and track the status of individual prospects progressing through the customer journey, it also enables the business to measure its progress towards some of its goals. Thinking back to the first tactic, you likely have sales targets as one of your organization-level goals. Perhaps you're looking to hit $10,000 in monthly recurring revenue (MRR). Your pipeline can help you to gauge whether you will reach that goal using the concept of estimated value.

Paying customers have an actual value to your business: if they pay you $1,000 each month then you know their exact value at present. Prospects in your pipeline who are not yet paying customers are not worth $1,000 to you now but are also not worth nothing. Their value is dependent on which stage in your pipeline they are in. For each stage of the funnel, you should have a standard likelihood of closing, which is represented as a percentage of the revenue they'd be worth if the deal closed. While not an exact science, this allows you to have a weighted portfolio of prospects and paying customers that more accurately represents the true value of your pipeline.

Larger, established organizations have historical data to determine the likelihood that a new lead will convert into a paying customer. Since you're still in the early days of your venture, you will need to create informed estimates.

If you estimate a 1% chance a lead will convert into a paying customer, then you can estimate their value to you at 1% of $1,000, or $10. If you have a potential customer who has already reviewed and red-lined a contract, you can estimate there is a 95% chance they will convert into a paying customer so their value would be 95% of $1,000, or $950.

DISCIPLINED ENTREPRENEURSHIP

REFER TO STEP

13

CUSTOMER ACQUISITION PROCESS

REFER TO STEP

18

SCALABLE REVENUE ENGINE

Calculating the sum of the estimated values of each potential customer in your pipeline will provide you with an estimate of your pipeline's overall value. If that overall estimated value is less than your organization-level goal then you know you need to take further action.

Increasing Estimated Value

So what do we do if our estimated value is less than the organization-level goal we have set? There are three approaches we can take to increase the estimated value of our pipeline.

First, we can look to increase the number of leads at the top of our sales funnel. Assuming a large enough TAM, this is simple to do as we can increase our investment in lead generation. By running larger or additional advertising campaigns, our value proposition gets in front of more people, which will generate additional leads even if we remain at the same conversion rate. Even better, we can continue refining both our messaging and our advertising targeting filters to achieve an even higher conversion rate. To maximize efficient usage of our resources, that means lots of small experiments to see which tweaks make a meaningful difference.

Second, we can improve our conversion rates from one stage of the pipeline to the next. Once we have initial leads in the funnel we can create additional touchpoints to reiterate our value proposition. For example, we could have a drip email campaign for leads that sends them a sequence of emails with messaging that builds on previous sends. Each subsequent email places an emphasis on different aspects of the value proposition. These might highlight customer success stories—assuming those exist yet—or offer different types of calls to action (begin a free trial, download a white paper, set up a consultation, get special exclusive pricing, attend a webinar/demo, etc.). Increasing the volume and variety of "carrots" should get more prospects engaged. Also, see where most leads stall or fall out of the pipeline and devote your attention and resources to understanding why that stage is mucking up the flow.

Finally, we can increase the speed at which leads move through the funnel. This requires converting leads to paying customers faster by optimizing sales and marketing techniques. Pressure test the funnel to see where friction points lie and figure out ways to minimize or eliminate them, such as reducing the number of required fields on forms or streamlining the procurement/payment process. Identify which stages might benefit from personal outreach over the phone or email to allay their concerns and create a repeatable process to make those connections. We can also try using time-sensitive offers for exclusive content, functionality, or pricing to get prospects off the fence.

The other angle of attack is revisiting who makes for a high-quality, qualified lead. For example, we might have thought teachers would be our primary customers for our educational software, but it's really administrators we need to be focused on. Or maybe we realized that a particular watering hole from Tactic 3, Market Research, isn't yielding good prospects so we should deemphasize that pool of individuals or maybe even remove them from consideration altogether. Even though we're shrinking the overall prospect pool with these edits, this refinement can save us from wasting resources on poor fits for the solution. Getting to "no" faster—whether it's their call or ours—helps us optimize our resource allocation to concentrate on folks with a higher likelihood of becoming buyers.

Building a Lead List

Your sales pipeline lets you visualize all the leads you are currently attempting to convert into paying customers. It starts with a lead list, which is a list of individuals—not companies—you're trying to acquire as customers.

Step 1: Identifying Target Accounts (B2B)

Your development of a lead list will often begin with a list of target companies or accounts if you are building a B2B business. You will see how this applies more closely to B2C businesses in step 2. Even B2C businesses may need to do some sort of sales to other businesses, however, and this step does apply when building a sales plan for attracting suppliers, channel partners, distribution partners, and other businesses that can help move yours forward. These targets should all be within your Beachhead Market at this point, otherwise you risk losing focus. You can curate a list of target companies by referring back to some of the watering holes you first visited.

An example of building a B2B lead list is the work we did at Oceanworks, as we built out sales campaigns. Our goal was driving commercial demand for recycled ocean plastic to reduce plastic pollution in our oceans at scale. In an effort to sell high volumes of recycled ocean plastics to brands interested in manufacturing and selling more sustainable products, we sought to build a lead list of organizations likely to purchase recycled ocean plastic from us.

We began by identifying the organizations who signed on as activators to the U.S. Plastics Pact, which brings together businesses and other organizations to work together towards scalable solutions that rethink the way we use plastics as materials to create a circular economy in the United States. This list provided us a starting point for brands most likely to buy bulk recycled plastic based on the public plastic commitments they had previously made.

DISCIPLINED
ENTREPRENEURSHIP

REFER TO STEP

2

BEACHHEAD
MARKET

Great Local Brands of
Ahold Delhaize | USA

The Association of
Plastic Recyclers

Partial list of activators (organizations) for the U.S. Plastics Pact.[1]

[1] https://usplasticspact.org/about/activators-of-the-u-s-plastics-pact/

Step 2: Identifying Individuals

DISCIPLINED
ENTREPRENEURSHIP

REFER TO STEP

3

END USER
PROFILE

REFER TO STEP

15

BUSINESS
MODEL

The next step—after identifying target companies if B2B—applies to new startups regardless of the business model. Whether choosing from the list of target companies or solely relying on your target End User Profile, build a list of individuals you can create value for. You can augment your poll of potential targets using social networking sites or services that provide lead list data.

For example, in the Oceanworks sales outreach, we built a lead list of individuals who worked at the organizations that had signed on to the U.S. Plastics Pact with job titles such as "VP of Sustainability." We used a lead list service to build a list of over 100 individuals with that job title at the Plastics Pact organizations and acquired email addresses that were helpful in our outreach.

Ultimately you want a list of individuals who you can contact with a specific reason why they should engage with you. There is a careful balance between lead lists that are too large and too small. Lead lists that are too large tend to include people on the fringes of resembling the End User Profile, or the profiles of others in the decision-making unit. When a lead list is too small, it is unlikely to yield meaningful results through outreach because of what are sure to be limited response rates.

This will become clear as you begin your outreach. It is important to remember that regardless of whether you are building a B2C or B2B business, the process of building a lead list also applies to building partnerships, sourcing vendors, and more.

Writing Compelling Content

DISCIPLINED
ENTREPRENEURSHIP

REFER TO STEP

8

QUANTiFiED
VALUE PROP

Before sending outreach to individuals from your lead list, think carefully about what you are sending them. There is an art to crafting compelling cold outreach that deserves your time and attention. Craft an email template including the following:

1. Compelling subject line to get a high open rate
2. Something personal and relevant to the recipient based on your research (this results in the highest response rates)
3. The reason why you are reaching out to this person specifically
4. An introduction to your quantified value proposition
5. A link to any relevant assets you've developed from Tactic 4
6. Your specific ask of the individual for the next steps

This message should be clear and concise. You might consider running it by end users from your PMR before sending it out to the masses from your lead list.

DISCIPLINED
ENTREPRENEURSHIP

REFER TO STEP

12

DECISION
MAKING UNIT

REFER TO STEP

23

PROOF DOGS WILL
EAT DOG FOOD

Outreach with Experiments

As with all of the tactics—and directly relevant to Tactic 5, Marketing—you can use outbound outreach as a means of experimenting. Similar to how you can test End User Profiles and value propositions using online advertising, you can do the same through your lead list creation and content.

You can develop three separate lead lists with different job titles, for example. In an effort to determine which individual at the companies from the U.S. Plastics Pact would be most likely to engage with us through our sales process, we ran an experiment with lead lists for the VP of Sustainability, VP of Marketing, and Materials Engineers. After sending outbound outreach to each, we had data to inform us of the ideal first point of contact at target companies.

Similarly, if you are working to find additional clarity on which quantified value proposition resonates best with your end users, you can craft variations of your content and review the results to determine which works best.

You can A/B test your outbound outreach email templates to find the best fit. These experiments should build off of each other, leveraging the learnings from the previous campaigns to design the most effective, repeatable process.

Compounding Communication Mediums

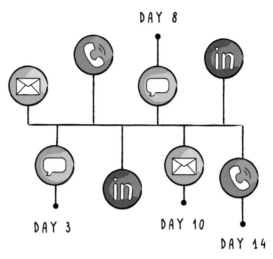

While you can write the most compelling content with your End User Profile and quantified value proposition locked in, that does not necessarily mean people will respond right away. You will need to send multiple follow-ups. Persistence wins.

There are a variety of tools that you can employ for follow-ups to make sure that you never miss a prospect. Rather than firing off emails from your Gmail account, you can instead leverage sales outreach tools such as Reply.io that will send automated follow-ups when prospects don't respond.

These follow-ups should be made roughly three to four days apart and you can combine mediums for the most impact. For example, you might start with a phone call, send a follow-up email, follow up a few days later with a LinkedIn message, and even send a text message if appropriate (and if you have a mobile phone number).

Outbound Sales Metrics

All your outbound sales efforts should be carefully tracked so you can measure what works and what doesn't. Track all of your outreach, including:

- Activities such as emails, phone calls, follow-ups, meetings, and demos
- Email open rates and response rates

- Click-through rates for links in outbound messages
- Meetings or product demos scheduled
- Number of touchpoints with a lead before they become a paying customer
- Number of open/closed qualified opportunities
- Average sales cycle time to move a lead through the pipeline to a paying customer

The data you gather through this outreach will be helpful for you to optimize the pipeline and prioritize sales and marketing activities based on their success rates, but you will also learn even more about your ideal customer profile.

Beyond Outbound Outreach: Sales for Startups

Building a lead list and sending outbound outreach to potential customers will help you to kickstart your sales processes. Through this tactic you will identify and engage potential customers, learn more about your customers, and begin crafting a repeatable process.

You will need to explore best practices to convert identified leads into paying customers—this will vary for each business. However, at the end of the day, you need to practice and become comfortable asking potential customers to pay you. Simply remember that they aren't doing you a favor by paying you. Instead, you are doing them a favor by providing value, which you should be compensated for.

EXAMPLE

Path Technologies

Sebastian Boyer and Tynan Dewes, both MIT Sloan MBA students, are the founders of Path Technologies, an EdTech startup aimed at fostering informed college and career choices for students. They employed the sales tactic to achieve one of the primary goals they had defined in Tactic 1, Goals, which was getting their machine learning software into three schools.

In implementing the sales tactic, Boyer and Dewes leveraged a state government website with a database of all schools in Massachusetts. They filtered this list to charter schools with students in grades 9–12, their Beachhead Market. They stored this information in Notion, a productivity tool chosen for its efficiency and flexibility, which they had aligned on in Tactic 2, Systems. They then went on each school's website and collected the contact information for three potential End User Profiles: 1) director-level school employees, 2) counselors, and 3) directors of technology. It was initially unclear which target group—decision-making directors, software-using counselors, or software-supervising tech directors—would be most responsive. The sales tactic ultimately doubled as a test to determine which would be the best first point of contact.

Boyer and Dewes then crafted compelling outreach emails and scheduled follow up emails with content focused on "Following up on previous email," "short meeting," and "want your opinion/thoughts." The structured process of building a lead list and executing outbound outreach to potential customers led the team to their first three customers. Lessons learned from this initial round of sales outreach informed subsequent communication strategies, enabling the expansion of their customer base and ultimately securing the first pilot customers.

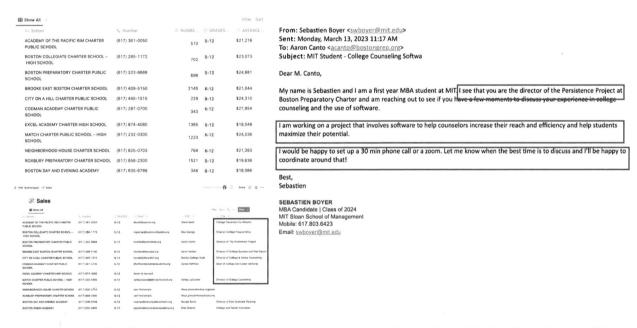

The Path team built a list of all relevant schools (target accounts) in their Beachhead Market. Next they identified the individuals who work for each school in the appropriate role. Their outreach to each of these individuals identified why they are reaching out and included a call to action.

Summary

Marketing can help you build the top of the funnel, and even close sales for B2C business and B2B businesses with a relatively low customer lifetime value (LTV), but sales will be needed for many businesses. The basics of conducting sales outreach with the goal of understanding the target recipient and testing value propositions includes building an extremely targeted lead list and reaching out. The best outreach combines a variety of communication mediums and includes A/B test experiments. This data will help to build confidence in the target customer profile and value proposition but more will be needed to close sales and expand the sales strategy. Now you can move forward confidently with a list of customers who want your refined quantified value proposition.

TOOLS OF THE TRADE

Lead List Generation

Clearbit (clearbit.com)

Hunter (hunter.io)

Demand Science (demandscience.com)

Seamless (seamless.ai)

Cognism (cognism.com)

Upwork (upwork.com)

Outreach Tracking

Apollo.io (apollo.io)

Outreach (outreach.io)

Reply.io (reply.io)

CRM (Customer Relationship Management)

HubSpot (hubspot.com/products/crm-control)

Pipedrive (pipedrive.com)

Streak (streak.com)

Nutshell (nutshell.com)

Salesforce (salesforce.com)

Close (close.com)

PROMPTS

1. Identify a list of companies you would like to target in your outreach.
2. Build out a lead list of individual contacts that look like your Persona.
3. Write an outreach campaign leveraging your quantified value prop.
4. Explore tools to automate outreach in your initial sales campaign.
5. Design your pipeline with the estimated value of prospects in your pipeline.
6. Evaluate how estimated value in your pipeline relates back to your goals/OKRs.
7. Push forward with online advertising tests/experiments from the last tactic.

WORKBOOK

Get the Startup Tactics Sales Workbook, which will help you build lead lists, craft compelling content, and send outreach to highly qualified target customers. Within you will find worksheets that include:

1. Targets: Define the companies and end users you are targeting with your outreach.
2. Data Collection: Determine how you will acquire the contact information for your leads.
3. Lead List: Organize your lead contact information into a convenient tracker.
4. Mediums: Explore the different ways you might get in contact with your leads.
5. Compelling Content: Craft the content you will send in your outreach.
6. Content Checklist: Review your content to ensure you have your bases covered.
7. Outreach Tooling: Evaluate tools you might use to automate your outreach.
8. Results: Track the success of experiments to improve with key metrics.

ADDITIONAL RESOURCES

→ **Get the Workbook!** Visit StartupTactics.net/sales

Product Development

After testing the market, you should have a homogeneous group of customers ready and waiting for your product, giving you the confidence to move forward with product development. You can now justify the investment of time and money in building your product since there are already people waiting to use it.

If you haven't successfully tested the market yet, consider whether building the product makes sense. You don't want to waste precious time and money building a product that might not have any paying customers. Remember, your focus is on building a business, not just a product.

Product development for early ventures should follow a structured process of roadmapping, designing, testing, and then engineering. Each of these are explored in the tactics within this stage.

Product Roadmap

Building Your Product's Roadmap

Entrepreneurs benefit from a balance between extremely detailed product plans and high-level direction to allow for flexibility in the product development process. Roadmapping helps set the plan for product development before ever building anything and that is where we will start.

The roadmap should translate the product vision into priorities for the product over time. The visual nature of a product roadmap allows you and your team to easily digest the next steps and it provides alignment for you and your team as to what is important in the product development process.

In This Tactic, You Will:

- Define your product vision and strategy to build alignment for yourself and your team.
- Build your initial product roadmap using the now, next, later approach.
- Refine the product roadmap to ensure alignment between product development and organization level goals.

Product Vision and Strategy

One of the many hats you'll wear as a founder is the role of product manager, where your job sits at the intersection of business, user experience, and technology. As a part of that job, you must set the product vision. The product vision defines what you hope for your product to achieve in the long term. The vision creates alignment so your team can build a roadmap that gets you to your shared goals.

From the product vision—which addresses the "what"—comes the product strategy, which represents the "how." The strategy is how you and your team will achieve the product vision. This strategy is the backing for product decision-making in support of the product vision. Your roadmap becomes the visual tool used to communicate the product strategy and to facilitate discussion about the product strategy as it evolves.

Roadmap Timeframe

Entrepreneurs have a lot of uncertainty in their product timelines given the rapidly evolving nature of their businesses. Rather than creating a big long list of features slotted into individual releases with delivery dates, take a more holistic approach to how best to communicate your priorities for the product you are building.

Consider the product roadmapping approach invented by Janna Barstow, the co-founder and CEO of ProdPad, which plots priorities on a relative timescale rather than an absolute one. She recognized the issues that arose with commitments to specific timeframes. Instead of specifying priorities by week or month, for example, Janna's method allows for prioritization on a now, next, and later timescale.[1]

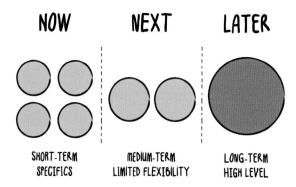

[1] Inspired by https://www.prodpad.com/blog/how-to-build-a-product-roadmap-everyone-understands/

You can make the best use of the now, next, and later timescale with this lens:

1. **Now:** Your highest-priority items, with specifics to provide clarity to the team
2. **Next:** Slightly less important items that don't have an urgent priority
3. **Later:** High-level items in this bucket to provide direction for the product but aren't necessarily hard commitments

Because new venture priorities can shift rapidly and commitments to specific timeframes can be problematic, avoid locking yourself into deadlines or setting unrealistic expectations. Your roadmap will not only be seen and used by your team, but also by external audiences in scenarios where a product roadmap might be shared with early customers to give them a sense of what to expect from the product. So don't provide more details or dates than are needed for the objective at hand, which may necessitate creating a more opaque, customer-friendly version of your roadmap that doesn't overcommit the business or reduce flexibility.

DISCIPLINED
ENTREPRENEURSHIP

REFER TO STEP
14
TAM FOR FOLLOW
ON MARKETS

What Belongs—and What Doesn't

A lot of product planning must happen, but it won't all be in your product roadmap. As a high-level tool to track your product priorities, it should not include nitty-gritty details such as the location of a button. Each item in your roadmap should move the needle for your product-related metrics at a high level. While the strategy will exist in the roadmap, you can translate the product strategy to specific actions and development items elsewhere. Your venture will tackle some of those more granular details in the next tactic, design.

In the "later" category you will likely include higher-level product guidance related to your follow-on markets, which are outlined in your product plan. These may be aimed at serving existing customers as well, with the intention of increasing the lifetime value of your customers.

REFER TO STEP
17
LIFE TIME
VALUE (LTV)

REFER TO STEP
24
PRODUCT
PLAN

Tying the Product Roadmap Back to Organizational Goals

Some of the organization-level goals we defined in the first tactic might have touched on the product. As you build out your product roadmap—and specifically the "now" section—you should be thinking about how to make sure the priorities included on your product roadmap tie back to your organization-level goals. The priorities set for your product must support the organization's efforts to hit those goals. To keep the roadmap aligned with top-level priorities, be sure to review the product roadmap whenever you make changes to your goals or OKRs and vice versa.

Summary

The product roadmap is a high-level product planning document that helps to communicate the product strategy and facilitate discussion. It should not be used as a product development "to-do" list and as such should not have intricate details about each feature to be built. Rather than using it as a release planner, consider using relative timescales knowing that priorities may change and your timeline may need to adjust. As you move forward with product development, the roadmap will keep everyone aligned and provide guidance on where the product is going.

TOOLS OF THE TRADE

Product Roadmaps

ProdPad (prodpad.com)

Craft.io (craft.io)

Airtable (airtable.com)

ProductPlan (productplan.com)

ProductBoard (productboard.com)

Aha (aha.io)

Airfocus (airfocus.com)

ClickUp (clickup.com)

Asana (asana.com)

Trello (trello.com)

Monday.com (monday.com)

PROMPTS

1. Write a product vision.
2. Identify best strategy to achieve your vision.
3. Articulate strategy in the form of a roadmap.
4. Connect roadmap to OKRs or other goals you have set.
5. Experiment with a product roadmapping tool.
6. Implement a process for reviewing new product ideas.
7. Identify jobs-to-be-done that are critical for your customers.
8. Integrate those jobs into your roadmap.

WORKBOOK

Get the Startup Tactics Product Roadmap Workbook, which will help you convert your mission into a product vision and then into a roadmap to guide your product development. Within you will find worksheets that include:

1. Product ideas: Jot down all initial features and/or functionalities you imagine.
2. Now: Prioritize the most urgent product features and provide additional definitions, context, and clarity.
3. Next and Later: Prioritize the less urgent product features and functionalities.
4. Goals: Review your product roadmap to ensure items align with your goals.

ADDITIONAL RESOURCES

→ **Get the Workbook!** Visit StartupTactics.net/product-roadmap

Design

Minimum Viable Business Product Design

The design process is where you should start product development as an entrepreneur because it allows you to iterate extremely quickly, which saves precious time. Entrepreneurs can build out the user experience they envision and test it with customers before ever writing a line of code or manufacturing physical products.

You have already tested elements of your business plan, and the Minimum Viable Business Product (MVBP) is a test of a product that actually provides value to your customer. More than that however, the MVBP is the simplest product you can provide that creates value for the customer, allows you to collect money from the customer (they actually pay for it!), and creates a feedback loop for improvement. If you've built a business plan then you likely already know what the MVBP will do. Now you can answer this question: What does the MVBP look like? All before you've actually built it.

With this initial design, you can test with users to refine things. These iteration cycles between design and user testing allow you to identify the product specifications most likely to succeed and most meaningful to end users before you begin building.

In This Tactic, You Will:

- Sketch the design of your product or solution based on your product roadmap in Tactic 7, Product Roadmap.

- Learn how to slowly increase the fidelity of your product design based on feedback you will receive in this tactic.
- Build clickable prototypes, which allow users to interact with the designs.
- Determine the appropriate amount of detail to include in higher-fidelity designs.

Migrating from Inquiry Mode to Advocacy Mode

When starting with PMR you must remain in inquiry mode and ask the questions that help you get to know your end users better than you know your best friends. Over time, you will begin a slow transition to advocacy mode. This is not a full shift once you gather a certain data point; it is instead an iterative process.

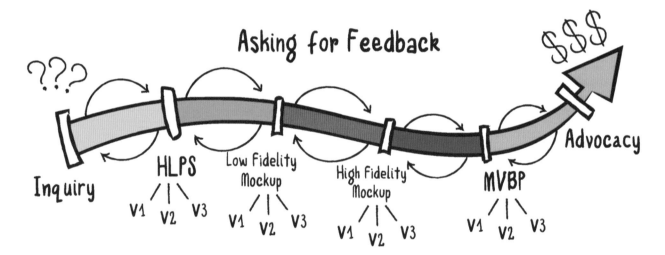

As you increase your product design's level of fidelity, begin socializing it with your end users through the user testing process. This tactic, design, is closely integrated with the next one, user testing. After creating your first product design you should user test it. Based on the feedback, you can improve it and add fidelity as you go.

Your confidence in the product design should continue increasing as you collect and incorporate more feedback, which will either confirm you're on the right path or potentially indicate the need for a shift. As fidelity increases, your confidence in the design should increase as well.

DISCIPLINED
ENTREPRENEURSHIP

REFER TO STEP

22

minimum viable
BUSINESS PRODUCT

Starting with a Sketch

Regardless of whether you are a seasoned, experienced designer or can barely draw a stick figure, it is always best to begin with a sketch. If you can draw out the product you envision, you can communicate it at a high level. The initial feedback you receive will help you to refine the overall structure of the product—whether it's software, hardware, or both—before you dive into the details. It's as simple as putting pen to paper.

Low-Fidelity to High-Fidelity

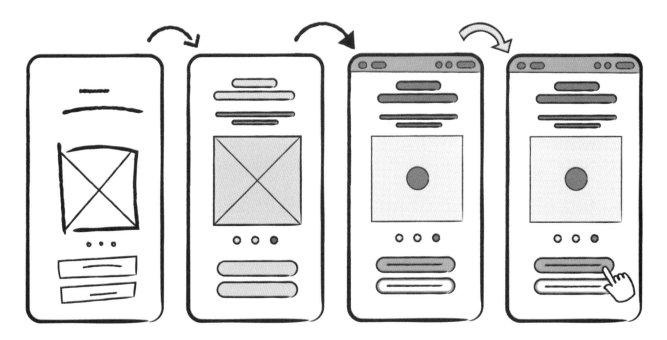

With some additional feedback from end users on your initial sketches, you can begin refining things and progress to a low-fidelity design. For software this may progress as a wireframe, mockup, and then clickable prototype. For hardware, on the other hand, you can consider starting with foam core, which you can mold into the shape of your product in no time at all with very little expense before progressing to laser cutting with acrylic and then 3D printing. In either case, your goal should be to start with the option that will provide the fastest time-to-design and lowest cost before moving forward. As you gain additional clarity on the product and increase the level of fidelity, continue bringing the product design back to end users for additional feedback.

Value of Sharing Low-Fidelity Designs with Customers

One question I often get when discussing sketches and low-fidelity product designs is around whether it is helpful to share an imperfect design with a PMR participant who might become an early customer. Entrepreneurs are usually worried it might scare off the prospect by not being perfect or making the venture seem unprofessional. Despite this discomfort, sharing an early product design, whether a sketch or low-fidelity mockup, can help you in two ways.

First, sharing low-fidelity product designs with potential future customers saves you time. You get their feedback before you have invested in building the full product, which provides invaluable insights that help you avoid building the wrong product.

Second, sharing low-fidelity product designs with potential future customers can help get them more bought in. Their insight into the early product design creates a sense of intimacy with the development of your product and business. They have a sneak peek into the future. As you incorporate their feedback through the user testing process, they will see the product evolve and that they played a role in that evolution. Their engagement in the product development process will create non-monetary buy-in, and as the product takes shape they begin to feel as if it is their own.

Components and Templates

As you transition from low-fidelity mockups to higher-fidelity ones, make use of different components and templates to advance your design as quickly as possible. Thinking back to the need to validate functionality rather than optimize precise design, your low-fidelity mockups can leverage predefined templates. Many of the popular product design tools provide a library of simple design elements such as navigation and buttons for software and physical components for hardware.

As fidelity increases, follow the same approach. Rather than construct your high-fidelity design, you can leverage existing templates already designed and built by others. Many of these templates are available on design marketplaces free of charge, while some come with a small cost. The cost will likely fall much lower than that required to build everything from scratch.

While using a template to build your high-fidelity design won't result in a completely unique design, your goal remains proving that you can provide value to end users as quickly as possible. You can create a unique design later based on the learnings from the templated design you begin with. Depending on the template, you may need to further customize it to add the functionality your product needs.

Building Clickable Prototypes for Software

As your confidence around a product design increases, for software products you can turn it into a lifelike product without investing in any engineering. Use advanced design tools to create functioning products that look and feel like a more polished product.

Clickable prototypes allow you to showcase your design in a web or mobile application interface. With multiple pages or screens, you can simulate user interactions as you would expect them to happen. For example, when a user clicks or taps a button on one screen, the clickable prototype can take them to the next page or screen you intend.

These clickable prototypes are incredibly fast to make and even faster to change, which increases the clock speed of your product development process. Ultimately, when it is time to proceed with engineering, your clickable prototypes will serve as your specification for what the product should look like and how it should function.

Avoiding Minute Details

Before you have a proven, built product, don't focus on small design details. At scale, with millions of users, small details can make a big difference. But at this point, you are looking to create value for end users that moves the needle. While still in the design process, your end users will use your product if the user interface is not perfect as long as you're actually creating the value promised.

A wonderful reminder of this is what ClassPass founder Payal Kadakia refers to as their "summer of buttons" in her 2020 *How I Built This* podcast interview from NPR. Kadakia recounts the summer of 2012 when Classtivity (as it was then known) didn't have any sign-ups, despite receiving significant press and offering free classes. They thought technology would fix everything and they spent time iterating on the colors, shapes, and sizes of the buttons on their web page.

The reality is that the business needed more primary market research before time was invested in perfecting the design. It's most likely that small design tweaks won't change the value an end user is able to extract from your product. Additional primary market research and an iterative design process could have saved them significant time and prevented the overinvestment in a product people wouldn't actually use a year and a half and $500,000 later.

Rather than spend time making small design tweaks, utilize user testing with an entrepreneurial lens to validate core product design decisions so, when you actually build the product, you build the right thing. Then, after confirming that you did, indeed, build the right thing, make those smaller design decisions to optimize for the masses.

EXAMPLES

catalan.ai

Andres Garza, MIT Sloan MBA '22, and Ishaan Grover, MIT Media Lab PhD '24, are the co-founders of catalan.ai. On a mission to empower small merchants with technology so they can better compete with larger competitors, they provide a dynamic pricing engine for e-commerce designed to maximize profits. Their offering is powered by technology developed by Grover using his eight-plus years of experience with machine learning models.

They faced a challenge, however, in demonstrating what the actual product would look like for merchants. Despite comprehensive technology behind the scenes, they still needed to design the product where customers could access the value their technology delivers. Their Beachhead Market of Shopify merchants made the initial product obvious: an app within the Shopify platform.

Garza and Grover designed the user experience as a prototype before coding the user interface for their Shopify app to show potential customers what the experience would look like from installing the application, configuring the dynamic pricing for each of the products they sell online, and viewing the results as their profit increased. The process started with hand sketches before progressing into low-fidelity wireframes with Balsamiq. They spent time testing the wireframes with customers before converting their revisions into a higher-fidelity prototype in Figma.

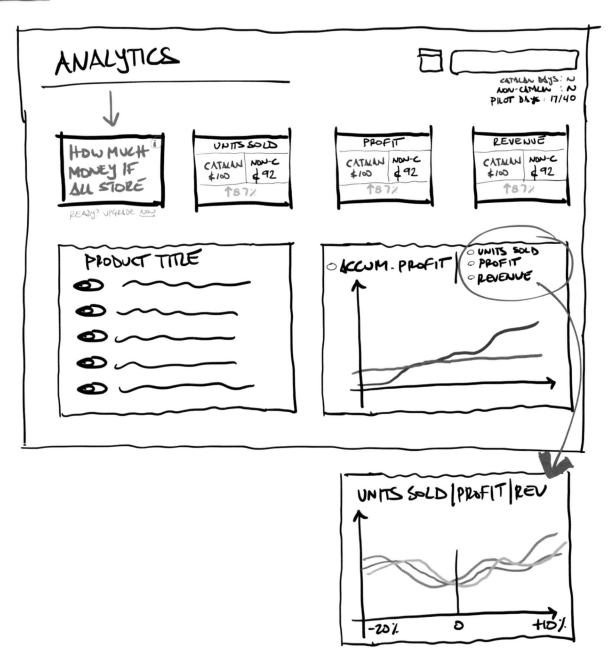

The Catalan team started their design process with a low-fidelity wireframe.

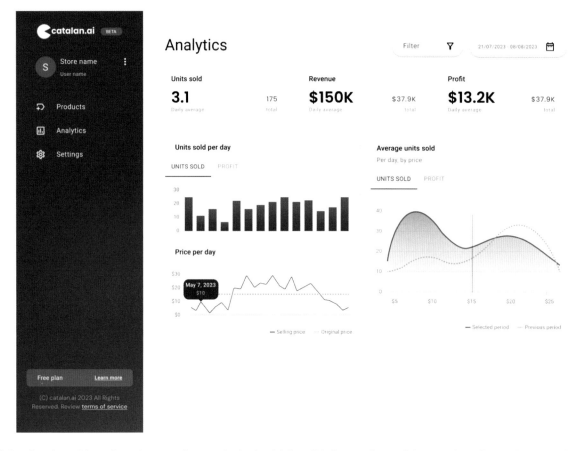

With feedback and iteration, the team began designing higher-fidelity versions of the user interface. This served to demonstrate what the product would look like to others and also informed the future of the product development process.

This design process allowed the pair of co-founders to show potential customers the product before having built it and move forward with user testing to refine the design. This approach saved them months of front-end engineering work.

While working through the design process, the pair also pushed forward with the development of their core technology—an integration with Shopify but no user interface. Their process was extremely manual. Garza would log in to their first pilot customer's Shopify store using the owner's login, check the products, and text Grover, who would then input product data into a command line terminal. The terminal would provide an updated price for the product, which Garza would manually update in Shopify. After 30 days of manual pricing using their artificial intelligence models, they saw a 7% profit lift for the store.

← → C 🔒 catalan.ai/admin_portal/3647209536/

Verbena Flores | Flores a Domicilio en Todo México - catalan day: false, days running: 42

back to portal
historical mean data
context hour
context weekday
context month

Sales History

All time:
catalan - profit: 11943.32, days: 17, mean per day: 702.5482352941176
non-catalan - profit: 15258.24, days: 25, mean per day: 610.3296
profit lift: 15.11%
Past 30 days:
catalan - profit: 11943.319999999998, days: 17, mean per day: 702.5482352941175
non-catalan - profit: 15258.24, days: 25, mean per day: 610.3296
profit lift: 15.11%
Past 7 days:
catalan - profit: 5809.35, days: 8, mean per day: 726.16875
non-catalan - profit: 5618.58, days: 8, mean per day: 702.3225
profit lift: 3.40%

date	catalan_day	total profit (v0b)	product	variant	variant_id	profit	units_sold	selling_rate	discount_percentage	selling_price	cost	pricing_version
2022-09-08	false	2044.58										
			1. Maria Félix Flores	Chico	31900418506855	629.58	1	1	0	749.99	120.41	v0_bridge
			La Vida en Rosa Flores	Extra grande (100 tallos)	25158416891968	1415	1	1	0	3200	1785	v0_bridge
2022-09-09	true	0										
2022-09-10	true	1252.8										
			La Vida en Rosa Flores	Chico(24 tallos)	14456101601344	1252.8	1	1.2	-20	1666.8	414	v0_bridge
2022-09-11	false	1204										
			La Vida en Rosa Flores	Grande (50 tallos)	18086067208256	1204	1	1	0	1999	795	v0_bridge
2022-09-12	true	664.6										
			1. Maria Félix Flores	Mediano	31900418539623	664.6	1	0.9249991572939021	7.5	823.24	158.64	v0_bridge
2022-09-13	true	1774.97										
			La Vida en Rosa Flores	Chico(24 tallos)	14456101601344	870.8199999999999	1	0.9249964002879769	7.5	1284.82	414	v0_bridge
			La Vida en Rosa Flores	Grande (50 tallos)	18086067208256	904.1500000000001	1	0.8500000000000001	15	1699.15	795	v0_bridge
2022-09-14	false	1204										
			La Vida en Rosa Flores	Grande (50 tallos)	18086067208256	1204	1	1	0	1999	795	v0_bridge
2022-09-15	true	0										
2022-09-16	false	1166										
			La Vida en Rosa Flores	Mediano (35 tallos)	18086067142720	1166	1	1	0	1700	534	v0_bridge
2022-09-17	false	0										

The early user interface was simple HTML and lacked design.

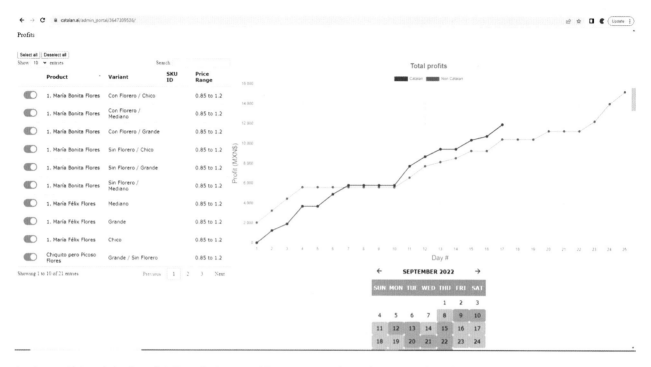

As they validated the low-fidelity wireframe with customers through user testing, the team began building the design into the user interface.

With this data point they had proven their ability to deliver on the quantified value proposition and moved forward with the development of their minimum viable business product with a less beautiful user interface. This interface served their next four pilot customers and provided proof points that helped in raising a pre-seed round of funding. Over time they improved their capabilities, providing up to a 46% profit lift for customers. It was then that the team proceeded with the development of the full product design.

PRAUD

P R A U D

Silvia Velasquez Casado, a dual-degree (MPA/MBA) student at the Harvard Kennedy School and MIT Sloan, has a background in human capital management but had not yet applied her skills in product design. After helping launch the neurodiversity hiring initiative at Goldman Sachs, she went on a mission to help the 85% share of autistic college graduates who remain unemployed and built a job-coaching platform to close the gap.

This platform served as a tool for both job coaches and students to go through the PRAUD curriculum, a 15-week lesson plan that equipped students with the tools they need to enter the job market. Going from resume building all the way through interviewing skills, job coaches would leverage this platform to have 1:1 weekly sessions with students and document their progress.

Based on PMR, Velasquez Casado organized what she knew about the user experience for her new app and began building a visual prototype using Figma, a design tool. With Figma, she could organize her thoughts into a visual that she could then transform into a clickable prototype for potential end users to navigate. Based on what she learned from sharing the clickable prototype with end users, she was able to revise the design rapidly without the need for a designer and prior to investing time and money in building out a functional product.

She tested this design with the job coaches and students and was able to gather all the feedback for product design before actually building the product. This was incredibly powerful because it allowed her team to know exactly what to build before spending any money on it.

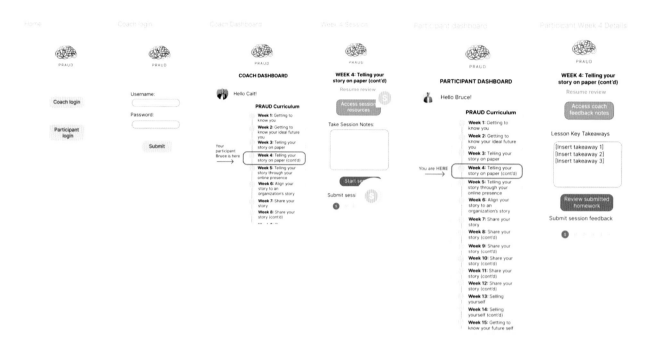

An early Figma clickable prototype of the user experience of the PRAUD application.

Summary

In order to run your product development process as efficiently as possible, you should start with product design rather than any engineering. The design should begin incredibly low fidelity with something as simple as a sketch. As you receive feedback you can iterate on the design and increase fidelity. The scale of the changes you will make at this stage in the product development process will be far more significant, so emphasizing design over engineering will allow you to save valuable time and money because it becomes much more time consuming, and therefore expensive, to reengineer rather than to redesign.

TOOLS OF THE TRADE

User Experience Design

    Figma (figma.com)

    Adobe XD (helpx.adobe.com/support/xd.html)

    Balsamiq (balsamiq.cloud)

    Axure (axure.com)

    Moqups (moqups.com)

    UXPin (uxpin.com)

    Marvel (marvelapp.com)

    Mockplus (mockplus.com)

    Sketch (sketch.com)

    InVision (invisionapp.com)

PROMPTS

1. Review your product roadmap to ensure it aligns with your overall goals
2. Grab a pen and piece of paper and draw out the design of your MVBP
3. Take your sketch and turn it into a low fidelity prototype
4. Enrich your low fidelity prototype by designing a full mockup
5. Create a clickable prototype you can share with potential end users
6. Establish your key hypotheses that you'll test with your MVBP

WORKBOOK

Get the Startup Tactics Design Workbook, which will help you design your product first with a sketch and then with a higher fidelity design. Within you will find worksheets that include:

1. Features: Determine which of the aspects of your product you will begin designing first.
2. Inspiration: Identify where you can look for design inspiration to help in your efforts.
3. Sketch: Start designing by putting pencil to paper to get your rough thoughts down.
4. Tools: Identify the best-fit design tool for your higher fidelity prototypes.
5. Templates: Save time by finding some templates that you can use to move faster.
6. Prototypes: Determine how you should connect the aspects of your design for a user.

ADDITIONAL RESOURCES

→ **Get the Workbook!** Visit StartupTactics.net/design

User Testing

Validating the Product Actually Works

In the early days of a new venture, the product changes both significantly and quickly. User testing is the natural follow-on to early PMR to iterate quickly in the product development process. Entrepreneurs can tweak a design much faster and at a lower cost than they can tweak code, which is why we spend so much time refining the product in this phase rather than when you're paying engineers to write and test code.

In This Tactic, You Will:

- Explore a new form of market research, user testing, to iterate on your designs.
- Source participants and write a script for your user testing sessions.
- Run live observed user testing sessions with end users of your solution.
- Learn to run unmonitored user tests and employ tools for unmonitored observation.
- Iterate on your design from Tactic 8 based on the insights gained from user testing.

PMR versus User Testing: One and the Same

User testing is a continuation of Tactic 3, Market Research. A form of PMR, user testing serves a purpose distinct from inquiry-based approaches. Unlike other PMR methods, user testing is closer to advocacy mode than inquiry mode. While you aren't advocating for your solution when conducting user testing studies, you are most certainly showing a proposed solution to gather feedback.

Moving forward with user testing should only come after extensive inquiry-based PMR. With user testing, you are gauging a user's ability to use (usability) your product and whether they get value out of it. In the early stages, user testing should be conducted exclusively on the product's design rather than a fully developed product.

Sourcing Participants

Before putting the product design in front of potential users, you must source a list of qualified participants. You should test exclusively with your target end users rather than conducting user tests with people around you, or your peers. Testing with individuals who are not your end users may confirm basic usability, but you are on the hunt for much more important insights.

Also keep in mind that your end user may perceive the product differently than your peers, family, or friends. I am often reminded of a track-and-trace mobile application I was developing for waste pickers in Southeast Asia to record their location while collecting plastic waste. These records would provide them with a financial benefit by proving the waste's origin authenticity.

We first mocked up a design for waste pickers to record the locations where they collect waste around an urban area. The design demonstrated a fallback method if the device was unable to provide geolocation. This fallback method displayed a map where the end user could drag a pin to indicate where they had collected the waste.

Basic user tests with others and those on our team led us to believe that this was a viable solution. It wasn't until we tested with potential end users and those who know our potential end users well that we learned the waste pickers we sought to empower with this mobile application were unfamiliar with the geospatial visual representation of Earth on a map. Only by testing with actual waste pickers in Southeast Asia were we able to learn a map was not the best approach for our end users.

You can build a list of qualified participants who resemble your end users by referring back to several sources:

1. Your initial PMR participants with whom you conducted interviews, observation, and immersion

2. Individuals you targeted and connected with through Tactic 5, Marketing, and Tactic 6, Sales

3. New individuals you can identify by revisiting the watering holes where you sourced your PMR participants

Building a Script

Similar to a PMR interview, you should go into any user test with a script. You shouldn't stick to the script exactly—because doing so can restrict your ability to collect new information that may surface—but instead use it as a guide you can return back to after fully exploring any user insights that arise. Following a script ensures you gather similar data points from all of your user tests so you can determine if there are common trends rather than giving every anecdotal nugget equal standing.

Your user testing script should also have a slightly different structure than an interview. A typical structure looks like this:

1. Background: Three to five questions to get to know the user testing participant that provide context for what you learn during the usability test that follows. These questions may resemble those of a PMR interview.

2. Usability Test: A series of tasks you want the end user to complete using your early product design. These are the tasks you anticipate an end user should be able to complete without direction based on the latest design, and the test you run will confirm whether that is, in fact, the case.

3. Wrap-Up: Reflective questions addressing what the end user likes or dislikes about the user experience overall, what they found most challenging, and what they would change or add if they had full control.

Overall, your script should make the user feel welcome. Let them know there are no wrong answers or actions. Encourage them to ask questions and narrate their experience as they go, highlighting anything that they enjoy, things that surprise them, and things that don't make sense or frustrate them. Remember: you're working to build a product your end users *love*, not a product they merely tolerate.

Live Observed Testing

There are multiple modalities for user testing. The first, and most impactful for early product development, is live observed testing. Live observed testing is, as the name implies, testing your design and/or product with the end users in real time, whether in-person or virtually. Through this process, you can observe how the user interacts with the product or product design prototype, allowing you to ask questions and pick up on nonverbal cues.

Live observed testing is most fruitful as a user testing method for early product development because it allows you to uncover the "why?" when things don't go quite as expected.

It provides incredibly valuable qualitative insights from the live interaction that you may not be able to uncover with alternate modalities (which generally help you understand only the "what"). In a live observed user test, I highly recommend having two people conducting the study: one to run the test and interact with the tester while another observes and takes notes.

Unmonitored User Tests

The most popular alternative to live observed testing is unmonitored user tests. Unmonitored user tests also help you understand what end users do with the product or product design prototype when there's no coaching or support available. They can be conducted using purpose-built software or through a simple video recording. In an unmonitored user test users are presented with the product or product design prototype and prompted to complete the tasks from your script. They are recorded while completing the tasks, giving you a record of what went well and where there is room for improvement.

One of the hardest parts of capturing the insights from unmonitored user tests is finding the time to watch the recordings. Many software tools can now provide you with highlights from the user tests, but you can still miss key insights that require context. The best approach to downloading the insights from unmonitored user tests comes from a former colleague at LogMeIn. As the UX designer on a cross-functional team, he championed user testing and led the charge of running our user tests. It's important that the entire team understand what is working and what isn't before moving forward with additional product development. To make sure the entire team understood the insights from our user tests, he gathered everyone together in front of the presentation screen on Friday afternoons, served cold mixtures of grain, hops, yeast, and water, and played the user test recordings for us to all learn from.

While I recommend live observed testing despite the fact that unmonitored user tests can be completed more efficiently, what is most important is that through either approach you empower the end user or tester to navigate the product or product design prototype themselves rather than presenting it to them or walking them through every action. Verbal feedback on a product presentation from an end user is far less insightful than watching an end user actually attempt to use a product themselves, ideally with them narrating their internal thoughts and how they're deciding what to do next.

Unmonitored Observation

Outside of directed user tests you can also leverage analytics tools such as Hotjar to monitor user actions in your website or other software product. With this tool, in just a few clicks, you can watch every customer's journey. You will see what they click, how long they spend on each page, and even where they move their mouse. You can watch these recordings of natural user interactions where, unlike unmonitored user tests, the users are not directed to complete specific tasks. From this form of observation you will learn a lot about the usability of your product. One of my students even described using tools like Hotjar as "being granted the keys to a hidden kingdom."

User Testing Metrics

Most insights from user testing may seem to be qualitative as they're all derived from intense, personalized sessions, but it can also be quantified, which is helpful for making data-driven product decisions. Qualitative feedback should be recorded in conjunction with quantitative metrics such as:

- Average time to complete each task
- Percent of testers who complete each task through the expected path

DISCIPLINED
ENTREPRENEURSHIP

REFER TO STEP

23

PROOF DOGS WILL
EAT DOG FOOD

- Percent of testers who complete each task through an unexpected path
- Number of clicks/taps/interactions to complete each task
- User feedback scores for each task

These metrics can be incredibly easy to collect using analytics software for finished software products, but they're just as important when conducting user tests on a product design prototype. While they can certainly be collected manually, there are also similar analytics software tools that allow you to collect the same information on prototypes. One such software tool is Maze, which collects key user testing metrics automatically when end users navigate a Figma clickable prototype.

Beyond the Tests Themselves

After conducting an adequate number of user tests, take your qualitative notes and quantitative metrics and summarize the findings into five to ten documented key takeaways. Based on these insights you can refine the product and conduct another round of user testing studies with a refined set of objectives. Much like PMR, user testing never ends. Learnings should be reviewed in the context of the product roadmap from Tactic 7. Any time you prepare to build a new feature or new product, you should always start by conducting user tests on the mockup or design.[1]

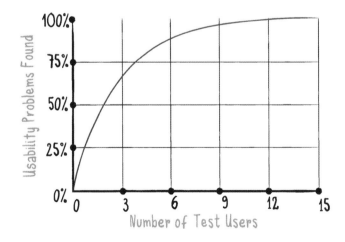

---

[1] https://nngroup.com/articles/why-you-only-need-to-test-with-5-users/

That sparks the question: how many user tests do I need to conduct? Research published by Jakob Nielsen and Thomas Landauer in their 1993 article, "A mathematical model of the finding of usability problems," shows that for usability tests specifically, you need no more than five users.[2] After testing with five users who match your target audience, you are likely to observe similar issues to the prior user tests and no longer generate new learnings. While you are looking to learn more than whether the product is usable during these early stages of product development, it is a more effective approach to run five tests, iterate on the design, then run five more tests.

User testing can involve much more than task-based observation studies, but these are the most effective in such an early stage of product development. You may follow on with additional user testing studies such as quantitative studies, card sorting, online session recording, eye tracking, and more.

EXAMPLES

Soundboard

Dedicated to supporting solo practitioners (such as therapists, college counselors, and career coaches) with software to improve the admin and back office operations, Nahel Rifai Burneo and Aaron Lewin founded Soundboard. As they began the product development process they advanced designs by slowly migrating from sketch to low-fidelity wireframe to higher-fidelity product. In this transition they spent a significant amount of time conducting user tests.

---

[2] https://dl.acm.org/doi/10.1145/169059.16916

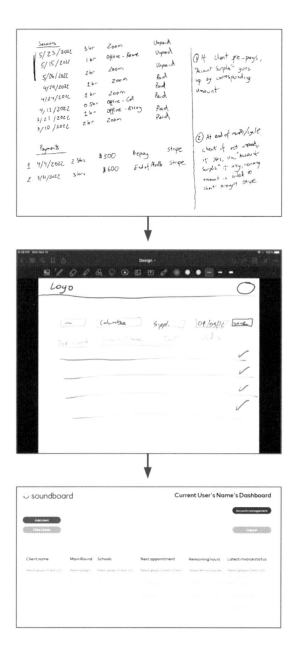

Based on the insights gained from user tests, the Soundboard team transformed their sketch into a low-fidelity wireframe and then into a polished mockup.

Soundboard Onboarding Instructions and Context

Part 1

1. **Open website** joinsoundboard.com/version-test
2. Create an account with your email
3. **Add a client** named "Martin Miller"
   a. Use martinmiller2023@gmail.com as client email
4. Open Martin Miller **client profile**
5. **Fill out** sample client information (as complete as you can)
6. Add sample **Client Notes**
7. Add a **Google Drive client folder** for this client
   a. Hint: Open your personal Google Drive and try to **get a folder link** and try to hook it up to the Soundboard Client Profile
   b. **Open** Google Drive Client Folder **from Soundboard**
8. Add a sample **SAT/GMAT test score**
9. Try to add **3 sample appointments** for this Client
10. The client **paid you** a certain amount by **Check**, try to **add that payment** to the system
11. Open the **invoice pdf** from that Check payment and then close it
12. Attempt to **Request a Payment** internally via Soundboard
    a. Ask Nahel/Aaron how to **"Skip this Form"** from Stripe
13. Once again, **Request a Payment** internally via Soundboard for $1,000
    a. **Modify the email message** being sent to the Client
14. **Upload a logo** for your business
    a. Use Google Images, search for **"Ivy Coach logo"** for the upload
15. Create a **second client** "Emily Smith"
    a. Use email "emily.soundboard@gmail.com"
16. **Request a Payment** from Martin Miller via Soundboard for **$500**
17. **Go back to initial CRM table** with your Clients
18. **Open the Dashboard**

Part 2

1. Receive **Aaron's computer** with Martin Miller's Gmail, **open email with Invoice**
2. Attempt to **pay first $1,000** invoice using a **credit card**
   a. Use credit card credentials:
      i.   CC #: 4242 4242 4242 4242
      ii. Exp: 06/26
      iii. CVV: 186
3. Attempt to pay second **$500 invoice** using **Instant Bank Transfer**
   a. Use a Bank of America Account
      i.   User: "user_good"
      ii. Password: "pass_good"
      iii. Text Code (if requested): "1234"

This is the list of actions that were presented to user testing participants in live observed test sessions.

Soundboard–Live Observed Testing Notes Session with A.S. (inc. step by step instructions)

Instructions Part 1

Registration
  • Last name entered instead of email

Adding Client
  • OK with Clicking Button
  • Billing type? Struggling a bit

Accessing Client
- She successfully clicks on Client to access client profile

Client Profile
- Did not fill out client profile directly
- Fills out notes properly by clicking Icon
- Attempts to add google folder but selects google docs as file type

Appointments and Payments
- Struggles to find Appointments and Payments Link but succeeds after 30 seconds
- OK with adding first appointment
- OK with second appointment
- OK with third appointment
  - Figures out how to add minutes properly

Payments
- Successfully adds manual payment and opens pdf
- Creates payment request successfully
  - After creating payment requests, clicks on email icon, confused
  - She missed the modify email message from payment request, she attempts to click the email icon to modify email

Account Settings
- She is able to find account settings
- She is able to upload a Logo

Creating another Client
- Adds a new fixed hour package client successfully (Emily)

Adding a payment Request for Martin
- Successfully goes back and creates an additional one without struggling much

Opens Dashboard Successfully

Part 2

Client received multiple emails, but she clicks to open portal successfully

Credit Card Payment
- No problem opening to pay by credit card

Bank Payment
- Error with bank payment from CD

Other General Notes
- Signed up using top right Sign up button

For each user testing session, the Soundboard team took detailed notes outlining how the participant was able to complete, or not complete, the tasks presented.

The major learning that team Soundboard had was that their user testing subjects need to be the same individuals who are the end users in their Beachhead Market. Initial testing was conducted with those close to the founders such as classmates at MIT Sloan. Knowing that their end users are not MIT Sloan students, they redesigned their user testing procedure to focus exclusively on testing with real potential end users: individuals who run one-person businesses. This new-found focus led to different findings than what they'd heard from classmates, which were much more helpful because they led to building the right features and redesigning to meet the unique needs of their users.

In addition, the Soundboard team was able to gather more detailed product feedback and richer PMR from potential end users after the testing session. A significant point made by several users was that they would be resistant to switching systems if the activation energy was too high, meaning they couldn't easily understand how to onboard their clients. Capitalizing on this insight, Soundboard decided to conduct further tests that included a fully prepopulated test client (i.e., Jane Doe). This approach would assist them in visualizing and brainstorming how they could store their own client information and billing data in Soundboard.

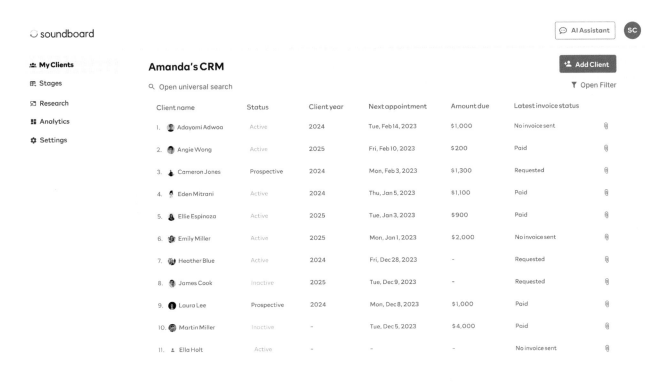

The Soundboard CRM system developed based on user testing feedback.

After allowing test users to first navigate the prepopulated test client, they completed the step-by-step instructions in roughly half the time.

All in all, the insights gained from their user testing sessions informed the changes that were made in the next iteration of the product with increasing fidelity—the right product for the right user.

Orbit

Neelesh Bagga, product manager for MIT Orbit, the one-stop shop for MIT entrepreneurs, led a user testing study on the new proposed design for the Orbit platform. The platform provides MIT student entrepreneurs access to everything the Institute has to offer, including events, courses, and other resources, along with connections to other entrepreneurs.

Prior to passing the design off to the engineer, Alfredo Garcia, Bagga ran a comprehensive study to identify any issues requiring revision before sinking any time or money into building it out.

Bagga sourced participants, designed a script, defined testing tasks, and conducted user testing sessions. He leveraged Maze—the design testing tool—to quantify some of the qualitative research he had conducted. During each user testing session, Bagga gave participants control and asked them to complete tasks, such as connecting with a fellow classmate within the clickable design prototype. Maze tracked every click from every participant and produced invaluable insights, including a full heatmap and data on time to completion, direct task completion success, and indirect successes of task completion. Participants were also asked to rate how easy they found a task on a scale of 1–5 after each task.

These metrics resemble those you would expect from analytics tools for fully built products but, with Bagga's approach, designer Navroop Sehmi and the rest of the team were able to revise the design based on concrete data before ever coding the changes into the product, thus saving valuable engineering time.

Usability Testing: Connect

Task: Connect with a fellow Sloanie

6.6s Avg. Time	64% Direct Success	36% Indirect Success	4.6/5 Easiness

Takeaways

- Users expressed a strong preference to search names via a Search bar and being able to narrow down by areas of interest

- In addition to current data points, user would like to look up work experience information

Users gravitated to use search bars and filters to find individuals.

Bagga and the MIT Orbit team used Maze to produce this report, which includes quantitative metrics about task completion and qualitative heat map visualizations based on a clickable Figma prototype.

Summary

A continuation of the market research from Tactic 3, user testing is not as simple as asking people for feedback. To run effective user tests, you should put your product designs in front of people who are your target end users. It is best to ask them to try the product and complete tasks that they should be able to. Their actions and feedback will inform how you should revise the designs to create the user experience that reduces friction for end users to extract value from the product. Eventually, once you have built the minimum viable business product, you can continue running user tests to continually refine the product.

TOOLS OF THE TRADE

Sourcing Participants

User Interviews (userinterviews.com)

Respondent.io (respondent.io)

Craigslist (craigslist.org)

UsabilityHub (usabilityhub.com/product/panel)

Wireframe and Prototype Testing

Maze (maze.co)

User Research Platforms

UserTesting (usertesting.com)

Dscout (dscout.com)

Lookback (lookback.com)

UXTweak (uxtweak.com)

Userlytics (userlytics.com)

UsabilityHub (usabilityhub.com/product/panel)

Product Analytics

Google Analytics (analytics.google.com)

Hotjar (hotjar.com)

Mixpanel (mixpanel.com)

Heap (heap.io)

Amplitude (amplitude.com)

CrazyEgg (crazyegg.com)

Mouseflow (mouseflow.com)

Live Session (livesession.io)

Lucky Orange (luckyorange.com)

PROMPTS

1. Review your product roadmap to ensure it aligns with your overall goals.
2. Design a user testing study to determine the next changes and enhancements for your product.
3. Recruit participants for your user testing study and get them scheduled.
4. Host a user test with someone you've validated through market testing.
5. Revise the UX design based on the learnings from your user testing study.
6. Revisit your product roadmap and adjust priorities based on your user testing study findings.
7. Add any new ideas from your user tests that warrant product development resources to your product roadmap or to the "parking lot" for future prioritization consideration.

WORKBOOK

Get the Startup Tactics User Testing Workbook, which will help you create a high-performing user testing plan, source participants to test your designs with, run the testing sessions, and interpret results. Within you will find worksheets, that include:

1. Research Goals: Have combined PMR and user testing goals.

2. Script and Tasks: Include the usability test tasks to evaluate.

3. Outreach: Craft messaging to potential participants to set expectations.

4. Participant Tracking and Scheduling: Track the tests you will run and ensure everything is set up well in advance and there are no scheduling conflicts with your team or the test subjects.

5. Insights Grid: Based on the tasks in your script, track their completion and ease.

6. Next Steps: After running your test, evaluate how to update your roadmap based on your learnings.

ADDITIONAL RESOURCES

→ **Get the Workbook!** Visit StartupTactics.net/user-testing

Engineering

Transitioning from Product Design to Development

Before onboarding a CTO or engineer, entrepreneurs can build out a preliminary product themselves and use it to generate additional customer feedback.

After validating your market, designing your product, and then testing it, it is time to proceed with an initial build. As a software engineer, I have unfortunately started with this tactic and bypassed the previous nine more than once, only to build a product searching for a business model instead of a business that offers a product. For hardware products there may be additional steps necessary, such as material selection, manufacturing identification, regulatory review, and so on, that need to be completed before or concurrently with this tactic.

Although the most technical of the tactics, day 0 engineering does not necessarily mean writing code or soldering circuit boards. As you transition from a product design to a fully developed product, you won't necessarily need to create the final product that will scale or sit on the shelves at big-box retailers. Instead, remember that you are building your Minimum Viable Business Product (MVBP).

In This Tactic, You Will:

- Determine how you will source technical talent if you do not already have it on your team.
- Build the minimum viable business product using the approach that requires the least amount of technology or code such as a no-code or low-code platform.
- Design your software architecture including front end, back end, database, and cloud technology.

Early Approaches to Technical Talent

It may not make sense to build the product yourself, particularly if you don't have a strong technical background and haven't yet hired any engineers. Each of the tactics within this book represents a "hat" or role that you are encouraged to wear yourself as an entrepreneur. The engineering and creation of your product is one role you should be familiar with so that you can, at minimum, communicate with more technical individuals if you are not one. There are a few approaches you can take to equipping your venture with the technical capabilities necessary to bring your product to market, as explained in the following sections.

DIY

The first approach is doing it yourself. If you are technical—or wish to learn the needed skills—you can invest in building the first version of the product on your own. But even if you possess the right technical chops, the hours and days you spend developing your product yourself will take away from the time and energy you could spend building the business.

While it can increase your iteration clock speed as you test and incorporate functionality, your bandwidth will be limited. If you are not technical, learning enough to bring your product to life will likely increase time to market, which may also be prohibitive.

Finding Your CTO

We'll explore hiring in more detail in the last tactic, Tactic 15, but you might consider hiring a technical resource such as a chief technology officer (CTO) or technical co-founder earlier. Bringing technical skills onto your team can be incredibly helpful, but it can also take a lot of time to recruit quality candidates.

Also consider the financial tradeoff, given that technical resources are expensive. Hiring a CTO will likely increase your burn rate and their overall compensation package may cut into your ownership of the business more significantly than you'd prefer.

Outsourcing

When building the product yourself or finding a CTO are not possible, you can also consider outsourcing. This might be to a freelancer, a contractor, or a development shop that builds products for other companies.

With this approach, you have a set project or engagement timeline and do not have to hire individual full-time resources yourself. In most cases, equity doesn't factor in and compensation is exclusively in cash due to the limited timespan of the engagement.

Weighing the Options

Remember that as your business grows, the decision to hire technical resources compared to outsourcing is not an either-or decision. In all likelihood, you will at some point complement in-house technical resources with freelancers, contractors, and/or outside dev shops.

In the short term, keep these things in mind:

1. You should have technical competencies on your team to round out the team's skills.

2. A full-time technical resource adds value to the team *and* to the business's value.

3. Freelancers, contractors, and dev shops do not have long-term commitments to the business, so significant technical debt (future cost of not fixing engineering problems now) is possible.

4. Routine maintenance becomes difficult without institutional knowledge, which is often lost when an engagement with a freelancer, contractor, or dev shop ends.

DISCIPLINED
ENTREPRENEURSHIP

REFER TO STEP

22

minimum viable
BUSINESS PRODUCT

In almost every case, hiring in-house, full-time, long-term technical talent for your team will best prepare your venture for success, but you may need to look to external resources to continue gaining momentum or get traction while you find the right people to bring aboard.

Also remember that your business and product will continue rapidly changing in these early years. As you learn from interactions with end users and customers, you will have to disseminate that information to your team, which is much faster and more seamless with full-time, long-term team members.

In most cases, you can and should build the MVBP yourself in the short term. This allows you to move forward with incredible speed, making changes in real time as you learn from your end users.

Levels of Technical Depth

You can advance the development of your MVBP by moving from a no-tech approach to a no/low-code approach, to building the full product. You might pick one of these approaches or you might move sequentially through them. This is not one-size-fits-all. You should be aware of each approach, build as little as you need to in order to create value for your end users, collect payment from your economic buyer, and create a feedback loop. These approaches apply mainly to software ventures, upon which this book focuses. You can adapt this progression for hardware ventures with an alternate approach that focuses on transitioning from rapid prototyping to first-generation product to full manufacturing.

No-Tech MVBP

The simplest MVBP is a no-tech approach that allows you to test your product with customers before building anything. With a no-tech approach, you can consider what solutions you might explore that can be created using physical materials (cardboard, for example) with the potential inclusion of off-the-shelf, consumer-grade technology. What is important here is not that no technology is *used*, but that no new technology is *created*. This is the fastest way to testing your key assumptions. Creating any new technology can set you back because updates and changes to that technology become more costly from both a time and a financial perspective.

DISCIPLINED
ENTREPRENEURSHIP

REFER TO STEP

21

KEY ASSUMPTION
TESTING

No-Code

When a no-tech MVBP yields positive results—or is simply not possible for your particular product—the next step is looking at no-code solutions to test your MVBP with end users. No-code engineering allows you to build working products using prebuilt functionality, which you configure using drag-and-drop interfaces. The visual configuration means you can bypass writing code for now, instead allowing the no-code system to generate your product for you. A no-code approach lets you accelerate your product's development cycle upfront while still being easy to change as needed.

Instead of rewriting hundreds of lines of code based on customer feedback, you can instead leverage the drag-and-drop interface for the no-code system to revise product functionality in as little as a few minutes. Prebuilt design components that come with no-code platforms are also big time savers. While the design of your no-code product may not directly match the design previously tested by end users, you can mimic the functionality knowing that when you "graduate" from the no-code solution you can completely customize the design.

While no-code provides a quick start, there are some tradeoffs. First, you can't introduce extremely custom functionalities in most cases. This is simply due to the fact that you're choosing from prebuilt components and functionality. Analyze whether you can actually deliver your unique quantified value proposition with the prebuilt functionality available. Second—while also a time saver because the prebuilt design components are standard—you won't have the ability to customize the design to your precise liking. And third, you will have an MVBP that will not necessarily scale. You may find that you hit performance limitations, customization barriers, and other challenges preventing you from growing with the no-code platform.

Low-Code

No-code platforms can be limiting. You are not always able to provide truly unique value because the level of customization is limited to standard functionality. In these cases, the next best option is leveraging low-code solutions. Low-code solutions let you leverage prebuilt components and functionality with the ability to write a small amount of code to introduce more robust, custom

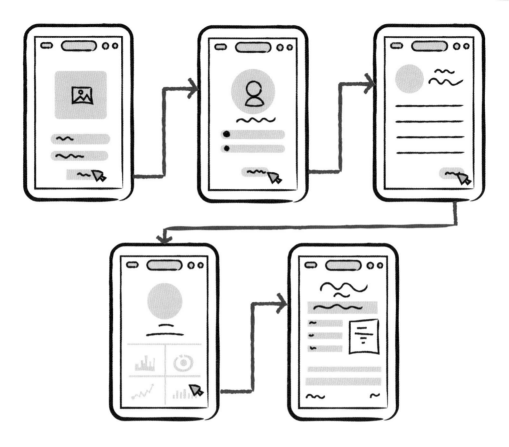

DISCIPLINED
ENTREPRENEURSHIP

REFER TO STEP

8

QUANTIFIED
VALUE PROP

functionality that delivers your unique quantified value proposition. With most low-code tools, you combine the drag-and-drop configuration interface with your own small, custom code snippets.

If your MVBP requires any kind of data manipulation, low-code is your likely starting point. The previously mentioned options don't offer that type of functionality, but low-code tools let you work with data in more detail.

One scenario entrepreneurs believe most often requires custom engineering is the introduction of artificial intelligence or machine learning. There are now a variety of low-code tools that tap into artificial intelligence and machine learning models without needing to build your product from scratch. These low-code tools leverage prebuilt models, which you can configure to provide unique value from the data in your product. The obvious tradeoff is that, in most cases, you do not own your models and must quickly graduate.

Leveling Up Beyond the MVBP

Eventually it will likely be time to "graduate" from no-tech, no-code, and/or low-code solutions. Leveraging these approaches for the engineering of your MVBP helps you accelerate initial development and make changes more quickly, but they have their limits and shortcomings as things get more complex or need to scale.

When is it time to graduate? You'll know the time has come to move on from these simpler approaches to engineering when you *need* product customization beyond what is possible, can no longer advance the product due to platform limitations, or find that your product breaks from performance issues encountered with too many users. These are good problems to have!

Software Architecture

While you may not write the software for your product yourself, you need to know enough about software architecture to effectively communicate with your product engineer or team. This applies for all software businesses and for most hardware businesses where there will be connectivity or a user interface. Following are some basic concepts you should understand.

Front End

The front end of your software application is the visual interface on a mobile phone, tablet, computer, or perhaps a custom hardware device that you have developed. The front end collects user inputs, conducts limited data processing, and interacts with the back end. The front end communicates information from the user to the back end, maintaining only very limited information in memory on the client device.

Back End

The back end collects information via an application programming interface (API) from the front end or other applications. It manages these information exchanges, manipulating data, sharing only what a user is authorized to see or know, and storing data in the database(s).

Databases

The back end retains only extremely limited data, storing most information in the database. The database is a long-term data store for structured information that will be needed in real-time or for scheduled processes. The database stores information about users, transactions, or other application-relevant information needed in the front end or for processing behind the scenes.

Cloud Providers

Your cloud provider serves your software from servers hosted in data centers around the world. The cloud provider allows you to leverage a variety of technologies for the front end, back end, and databases. There are a variety of cloud providers that each provide access to servers, but the unique attributes that might draw you to one provider versus another as a startup may be quite different than those that might be attractive for a larger organization (uptime and pricing). As a startup, you might choose one cloud provider over another for access to value-add engineering resources such as built-in models and technology services offered as APIs.

Case Example: Dignitize

During her time working in supply chain responsibility, Olivia Wold learned that one in five workers around the world work full-time yet don't make a living wage. While many firms are working towards ethical wages, Wold discovered that they don't have the software tools to collect and analyze wage data across their supply chains, so she founded Dignitize with some classmates at MIT.

Dignitize is a software solution that enables firms to easily collect and analyze worker data from suppliers to increase transparency and provides actionable, data-driven recommendations on how to achieve living wages for workers. Focused on their Beachhead Market—the apparel industry—they planned to scale to consumer packaged goods, food, and electronics—all industries investing heavily in social responsibility.

After conducting extensive PMR and market testing, Wold and her team decided to build out their MVBP using Bubble, a no-code platform for app development. Bubble allowed Dignitize to rapidly develop an application for brands to manage supplier communication, collect wage data, and view insights and recommendations on a dashboard. As their business needs evolved, making changes to the application required very little time because they built the product using no-code to start, with no engineering required. Making updates was as simple as point and click. Wold—who does not have a technical background—was able to build out a usable version of the app in a matter of weeks, instead of finding a technical co-founder in the early stages or spending money to outsource an engineering solution.

This MVBP was developed by Wold using the no-code application development platform Bubble.

Summary

There are several options to sourcing technical talent for your team and you should build a plan for the approach that will be right for your business. In the meantime, you can use your own skills to build a minimum viable business product that incorporates the features prioritized from your user testing in Tactic 9. No-code and low-code platforms can help you to build and refine your product. Once you have people using your product you will need to advance the product beyond these technologies and you can build a proposed software architecture that your engineering team will use.

TOOLS OF THE TRADE

No-Code Platforms

Bubble (bubble.io)

Thunkable (thunkable.com)

Builder.ai (builder.ai)

Softr (softr.io)

AppGyver (appgyver.com)

Glide (glideapps.com)

Low-Code Platforms

Kissflow (kissflow.com)

8base (8base.com)

n8n (n8n.io)

Outsystems (outsystems.com)

Zoho Creator (zoho.com/creator)

Creatio (creatio.com)

Internal (internal.io)

Retool (retool.com)

Wavemaker (wavemaker.com)

Reify (reify.com)

Unqork (unqork.com)

No-Code AI/ML Platforms

Stack AI (stack-ai.com)

Obviously.ai (obviously.ai)

Lobe (lobe.ai)

Clarifai (clarifai.com)

MonkeyLearn (monkeylearn.com)

Akkio (akkio.com)

DataRobot (datarobot.com)

Levity (levity.ai)

Frontend Technologies

HTML (developer.mozilla.org/en-US/docs/Web/HTML)

CSS (w3.org/Style/CSS/Overview.en.html)

Javascript (developer.mozilla.org/en-US/docs/Web/JavaScript)

React (react.dev)

Angular (angularjs.org)

Vue.js (vuejs.org)

Swift (developer.apple.com/swift/)

Backend Technologies

Ruby (ruby-lang.org)

Node.js (nodejs.org)

Python (python.org)

Go (go.dev)

Java (java.com)

PHP (php.net)

Database Technologies

MySQL (mysql.com)

PostgreSQL (postgresql.org)

MongoDB (mongodb.com)

Firebase (firebase.google.com)

Cloud Providers

Amazon Web Services (AWS) (aws.amazon.com)

Google Cloud (cloud.google.com)

IBM Cloud (ibm.com/cloud/)

Oracle Cloud (oracle.com/cloud/)

Microsoft Azure (azure.microsoft.com)

PROMPTS

1. Establish your key hypotheses that you'll test with your MVBP.
2. Grab a pen and piece of paper and draw out the "design" of your MVBP.
3. Turn your mockup into a usable product using a low-code or no-code tool.
4. Identify the best path forward for you and your team to acquire technical resources, whether that is recruiting a technical co-founder or outsourcing.
5. Find individuals who might be a good fit for your team (if recruiting).
6. Map out your technical architecture to easily communicate it to a technical co-founder or freelancer you recruit to work with you.

WORKBOOK

Get the Startup Tactics Engineering Workbook, which will help you identify the appropriate technology to use to build your MVBP and map our your engineering architecture. Within you will find worksheets that include:

1. No-Code Tools: Evaluate potential no-code tools you can leverage.
2. Low-Code: Identify the unique value add you can introduce with low-code.
3. Front End: Map out the front end of your system and identify the right technology.
4. Back End: Map out the back end of your system and identify the right technology.
5. Database: Design a simplistic database and identify the right technology.
6. Data Design: Design the simplest form of your database in a spreadsheet.
7. Talent: Evaluate the best-fit approach to hiring, outsourcing, or a DIY approach.

ADDITIONAL RESOURCES

→ **Get the Workbook!** Visit StartupTactics.net/engineering

Resource Acquisition

With goals set, the market tested, and an early product already developed, you now have *traction*. This increases your ability to acquire additional resources to continue building your business because you have proof points and success stories to leverage. You can augment your two most precious resources as an entrepreneur—time and money—by acquiring more people for your team and amassing funds in the bank, respectively. In most cases, before hiring additional team members beyond the founding team, you will need to fundraise so you can pay the new team members.

To acquire additional resources, particularly financial ones, you must incorporate, prepare your financial plan, and develop a pitch deck to communicate your business plan, traction thus far, and goals for the business moving forward.

Resource-rich businesses are often considered to be successful, especially because they are regularly covered in the news headlines. But we must also remember to take care in acquiring additional resources. It is unwise to take money just because it is available, and you shouldn't hire until you need to. These can lead to diluting your ownership in your business and wasting cash. We need more resources as entrepreneurs, but we still need to be *resourceful*. Remember, this book is about being and staying scrappy.

TACTIC 11

Legal

Incorporation and Legal Documents for Your Startup

When the time is right, incorporating your business is a box that you must check to operate legally. Unlike other tactics, you should consult an attorney (because I am not one). This is how I preface all meetings where I advise entrepreneurs when a legal topic arises. The views below represent my own personal experience but not legal advice.

In This Tactic, You Will:

- Determine when it is the right time for you to incorporate your venture.
- Explore the considerations for entity structuring.
- Align on the equity split with your co-founders.
- Learn many of the legal terms that you will encounter in the first few years of your venture.

When to Incorporate

There is a time and place to incorporate and it isn't necessarily day 0. Entrepreneurs must be aware of the indicators that it is time to incorporate to protect themselves and their businesses.

It can be too early to incorporate your new venture, but you can also wait too long. If you did miss the ideal window for incorporation, for first-time entrepreneurs this becomes obvious when problems arise.

Determining how early to incorporate requires an understanding of balance. In my personal experience, it can hurt you to incorporate too early. Incorporating too early introduces significant expense and time better spent elsewhere building the business. So when is the right time to incorporate? I have found that reaching any of these milestones is an indication you should incorporate:

- Hiring: Once you hire someone onto your team, you will want to have the proper paperwork set up in place to protect the business and formalize the relationship.
- Sales: In most cases, if you are collecting money from a customer in exchange for a product or service, it is wise to incorporate to protect yourself.
- Raising Venture Capital Funds: Investors will need a corporate entity to commit their funds to and complete paperwork with.
- Banking: Opening a business bank account usually requires incorporation.
- IP: If you are creating or filing for any intellectual property, you will want it assigned to the corporate entity rather than any individual.

Keep in mind that you are incorporating the venture, or business, not the idea or team. The idea and/or team will likely change.

Entity Structure

For most new innovation-driven enterprises seeking to incorporate in the United States, there are two entity structures that are simplest, most straightforward, and most appealing to investors. The first is an LLC, or limited liability company, which serves founders with the benefits of sole proprietorships including pass-through income and loss, but also offers the legal protection that is provided by a corporation. The second entity structure is a corporation, often referred to as a C-corp, which protects owners personally so they avoid the company's liability. C-corps are what investors generally look to invest in because they are less interested in business where the income and loss pass through directly to owners. For those who elect to incorporate as an LLC and subsequently fundraise, investors will often request that the entity convert to a C-corporation before the investment closes, which incurs additional expense.

The question also arises where the organization should be formed legally. In most cases, for an innovation-driven venture formed in the United States a C-corporation formed in the state of Delaware is desirable because most people are familiar with this default structure. The set up process is straightforward and provides a significant amount of flexibility. For those operating elsewhere registration with each state in which the business has employees may be necessary.

For international founders there are additional considerations regarding where the company should be headquartered, visa restrictions, and tax implications that must be researched. For entrepreneurs setting up businesses in other countries there will be additional considerations that need to be explored and taken into account.

At the end of the day it is up to you to do your research, consult legal counsel, and make the decision that makes the most sense for your business both now and in the future should you seek out venture capital.

Considerations for the Team

Your co-founders must also engage in the incorporation process. Each member of the co-founding team should be involved in equity discussions. The initial equity for the business will, in most cases, be split up among the co-founders—not necessarily evenly—but you should also plan for your employees and/or future team members as well.

Depending on your venture's stage, you will want to reserve 10–30% of your equity for an option pool. This option pool is a chunk of shares in the company set aside so that it can be issued to employees, advisors, or others who provide value to the company in the future. Equity compensation is an important component of total compensation for new ventures because it helps you to attract and retain top talent and ensure that talent is aligned with the success of the venture. Setting up an option pool sets aside some portion of the company to be owned by employees who have not yet been hired without requiring the dilution of existing owners each time a new employee is hired.

Equity Split

There are important considerations to be made in determining how much of the company each co-founder will own and a variety of dimensions that must be evaluated. Many entrepreneurs look to others for input on how to split up the ownership of their new venture. The reality is that there is no perfect comparison or benchmark. Even with all of the external input, you can still wind up with a situation in which one co-founder does not feel like it was a fair split.

You're on the hunt for a split in which each founder feels both appropriately compensated and incentivized now and in the future. Considerations for this calculation include time already committed to the venture, leadership roles, time commitment moving forward, any financial investment in the business, and relevant background experience. While short-term, forward-looking commitments might be reduced because of another job, schooling, or source of income, remember that the development of a new venture is a marathon, not a sprint, and equity should reflect the long-term timeline.

Should you have an equal split? There is wild debate on this topic. While an equal split allows everyone on the early co-founding team to feel equal ownership, it can also cause complications in decision-making when there are an even number of co-founders. In these instances, should you choose to move forward with an equal equity split, I recommend aligning as a team on a key decision-maker. For some ventures, this may be the formal directors or officers of the corporation. This alignment allows you to move quickly as a venture so the pace of development does not slow down when an agreement can't be reached.

Equity splits are determined at incorporation but have a lasting impact for those building the business. Everyone, including all founders, should have vesting schedules in place. These vesting schedules help to reward those who take the risk of joining the new venture but also reward those who stick around. Typical vesting occurs over four years and may include a cliff after one year. A typical vesting schedule would see 25% of equity vest at the one-year mark and 1/48 of the equity each month thereafter until the four-year mark. Vesting protects the company, and protects you as a founder, should someone depart earlier than expected.

In your next fundraise you are sure to run into trouble if, for example, a vesting schedule was not in place for a co-founder who has 33% equity but has decided to take on a full-time job working in consulting with a bigger paycheck. Your ability to fundraise will be impacted and it's likely that your motivation to push the business forward will falter because your efforts are rewarding your former co-founder who has since left you to fend for yourself.

Representation

As you move through the incorporation process you will need to determine whether to seek legal representation. I always recommend new ventures to find a long-term legal partner to work with. However, a variety of services have emerged to help entrepreneurs incorporate their ventures. These services are offered largely online, collect required information through web forms, and help complete all governmental filings and organization paperwork.

While these services can expedite the incorporation process and limit upfront expenses, there are drawbacks. These services are largely templatized and, as a result, may require significant follow-up with a legal professional, which can be costly. Additionally, these services do not provide the synchronous education you may receive from a legal professional. Some services offer ad-hoc support but not always from people qualified to provide legal guidance. You need a reliable resource to assist you not only to create your paperwork but to understand it as well. Incorporating using an online service can save money in the short term, but can also increase legal expenses in the medium to long term.

A trusted, long-term legal partner for your new venture can bring incredible value and their fees will likely reflect the value they provide. A trusted legal partner can help you understand small details that may make or break a financing, for example. Depending on the legal professional you engage with, their experience, specialty, and location, you will find that their fees can range from $200 to $1,500 per hour. Because of this, you should meet with a number of different individuals or firms so that you have different options to choose from. While this specifically applies to lawyers, you should also follow the same approach for other professional service providers and vendors in general.

Incorporating is just one part of the venture's legal journey. Often incorporation is a project through which entrepreneurs and lawyers build the foundation of their relationship. But what comes next is where that relationship is tested and becomes so valuable, because the legal partner you choose will be there through the first round of fundraising, hiring, and firing, among other future milestones.

Legalese: A Startup Glossary

You should be familiar with various legal, or legal- and fundraising-related terms as an entrepreneur so you're prepared when you encounter them in practice. You should consult with your trusted legal partner when you need to use these terms in any formal sense to ensure that they're being applied properly, but to help you understand them better, they're provided here in general layperson's terms:

409A: Appraisal from a third-party of the fair market value of a private company's stock

Accelerated Vesting: Vesting that occurs more quickly than the initially planned vesting schedule and is most common upon an exit, such as an IPO or sale of the company

Accredited Investor: Individuals who are eligible to invest in early-stage companies based on certain qualifications

Acquisition: The purchase of a venture by another organization

Angel Investor: Private individual investors who invest cash in a business in exchange for equity or convertible debt/note

Authorized Shares: The maximum number of shares that a company can issue to investors legally as defined by the shareholders or board of directors

Board Consent: Permission provided by the board of directors needed for startups to take certain actions (Actions are usually outlined in the company's bylaws or operating agreement.)

Board Observer: Individuals who are granted permission to attend and observe board meetings but who do not have voting power

Bridge Financing: Short-term financing needed to holdover a company until a more significant round of financing can be closed

Capital Call: When an investment firm requests committed capital from limited partners

Capitalization Table: Document detailing the individuals who own the company and the amount of equity in the company they have

Clawback: Provides investors the right to reclaim money, equity, or options from founders or employees if certain events occur

Cliff (Vesting): A period of time when vesting does not occur until a set date when a significant amount of stock or options vest immediately

Copyright: Protection of original work that has been created and/or published providing an exclusive right to reproduce and distribute; protects only the work, not concepts that inform the work

Common Stock: A class of stock representing ownership of a company

Convertible Debt/Note: Loan from an investor that is agreed upfront to be repaid in the form of stock in the future

Corporate Governance: The way a company is governed, including who makes decisions, who has responsibilities, and who has power

Design Patent: A form of intellectual property protection for visual elements of a manufactured item

Double Trigger Acceleration: Acceleration of vesting upon the occurrence of two separate events, such as a sale of the company and involuntary firing

Down Round: A fundraise and financing of the company in which stock is sold at a price less than that in the previous round of financing

EIN: Unique identifying number assigned to an organization

Exercise: To choose to make use of stock options by purchasing shares of a company's stock at a predefined price

Exercise Price: The price at which an individual can exercise their options to purchase company stock, also known as the strike price

Fiduciary Duty: Responsibilities that are formal legal obligations requiring founders always to act in the best interest of the company before their own best interest

Indemnification: Legal term signifying an agreement by one party to cover any losses incurred by another party to a third party

Indemnification Cap: Limit of liability at a certain amount

Independent Director: Individual who is external to the company and on the board of directors to provide a unique perspective

Intellectual Property (IP): Intangible property including inventions, art, names, and other works of intellect that can be protected

Letter of Intent (LOI): Nonbinding letter written to outline terms to which parties intend to agree to and enter into definitive agreement under

Licensing Agreement: Legal contract providing one party the right to use, produce, or sell products or intellectual property owned by another

Liquidation Preference: Order in which payouts are made to different parties should a company liquidate

Material Transfer Agreement (MTA): Contract governing the transfer of research from one organization to another, used to protect rights to intellectual property

Noncompete: Element of an employment agreement preventing an individual from working for a competing business

Nonprovisional Patent: Utility patent that is reviewed and, if issued, has a 20-year lifespan

Non-solicitation: Component of a contract that prevents employees from recruiting clients, suppliers, employees, or using information for the benefit of other organizations

Officer: An individual appointed to the organization by the board who also reports to the board

Option Pool: Block of stock in the company reserved for employees

Outstanding Shares: Total number of shares in a company that are owned by the shareholders

Par Value: Lowest price for which a company can sell stock

Preferred Stock: Class of shares in a company that offer advantages over common stock owned by the founders and employees, such as protective provisions and preference in the event of liquidation

Price Per Share: Value of each share of stock in a company usually calculated by dividing the pre-money valuation by the number of shares outstanding

Pro Rata: Investor rights to maintain their ownership of a company when it raises additional funding by participating in future rounds

Promissory Note: Legal document outlining an obligation to repay a loan over a certain period of time

Provisional Patent: A patent that will never be examined and has a short lifespan of only 12 months, during which a nonprovisional patent must be filed

Qualified Financing: Amount of money that must be raised for convertible debt/note to convert into stock in the company

Registered Agent: Individual or business responsible for representing a company in any communication with the government

Restricted Stock: Stock in the company that are subject to vesting

SAFE Note: An alternative to convertible notes designed for simplicity with straightforward, standard language

Service Mark: Registered trademarks that protect identification of services provided by a company

Single Trigger Acceleration: Immediate vesting upon the occurrence of one event such as an acquisition

Stock Options: Right to purchase a set amount of stock in a company at a predetermined price generally granted to employees, advisors, and/or contractors

Strike Price: Predetermined price paid by an option holder in exchange for stock in a company

Tag Along Rights: Liquidity protections provided to minority shareholders should majority shareholders choose to sell out

Term Sheet: Document that outlines the terms and conditions for an investment in a company

Trademark: Protection of identifying marks that distinguish products and services of one company from those of others

Utility Patent: Patent for intention of a new process, machine, manufacturer, composition, or improvement

Valuation: Value of a startup business impacted by business performance and the market in which the company operates

Vesting: Process of gaining ownership of stock or options in a company

Vesting Schedule: Outline of the periods of time over which amounts of stock or options in a company become vested

Warrant: Similar to stock options, warrants provide a party with the right to purchase a number of shares in the future at a predefined price but are issued to banks or investors as a part of a financial transaction rather than to employees, advisors, or contractors

---

Legal Documents

You will need a variety of documents for your incorporation and for your early entrepreneurial activities. These documents can often be pulled "off-the-shelf" from template libraries, but they might need customization and a lawyer will be helpful in that process. Some of the legal documents you will need in the early stages of building your business include:

- Charter Documents: Legal documents filed with the government to document the creation of a new entity, your business (For a corporation this is the Articles of Incorporation and for an LLC this is the Articles of Organization or Certificate of Formation.)

- Internal Documentation: Internal documents that outline how the organization is governed (For a corporation these are the bylaws and for an LLC this refers to the operating agreement.)

- Shareholders Agreement: Legal document that spells out the rules for running the organization and the shareholders' relationship with the organization

- Stock Purchase Agreement: Legal contract that documents terms and conditions related to the sale of stock in the company

- 83(b) Election: Letter to the IRS in the USA indicating that you would like to be taxed on company stock when you purchase it rather than when it vests

- Intellectual Property Assignment Agreement: Contract that assigns an owner's intellectual property to the organization, protecting the company should the individual leave in the future (Every employee and contractor should sign one.)

- Nondisclosure Agreement (NDA): Legal contract that protects confidential and sensitive information from being shared

- Offer Letters and Employment Contracts: Legal documents that, respectively, extend an offer of employment and outline terms and conditions for employment

I cannot emphasize strongly enough that you need to file your 83(b) elections. These elections must be filed soon after incorporation and will come into play in the future from a taxation perspective. Neglecting to file these elections can have significant future financial implications.

This is not professional legal or financial advice. Consulting a professional legal or financial advisor about your particular circumstances is best.

Summary

You should incorporate when you have hit a certain milestone that necessitates you have a formal entity. This will provide protections and a formal entity so that you can conduct business. At this point you and your co-founding team will need to have alignment on ownership of the business in order to draft and file the appropriate paperwork. As you build your business you will encounter a variety of legal terms that you may not be familiar with. The legal side of building a new business is an area where you should consult legal representation.

TOOLS OF THE TRADE

Incorporation Services

    Stripe Atlas (atlas.stripe.com)

    Clerky (clerky.com)

    Shoobx (shoobx.com)

    Gust Launch (gust.com/launch)

    Doola (doola.com)

    Savvi Legal (savvi.legal)

    WilmerHale (launch.wilmerhale.com)

Legal Templates

    Cooley Go (cooleygo.com)

    WilmerHale Launch (launch.wilmerhale.com)

    Goodwin Founders Workbench (foundersworkbench.com)

    YC Sales Agreement (ycombinator.com/sales_agreement)

    YC SAFE Financing Documents (ycombinator.com/documents)

Cap Table

    Carta (carta.com)

    Pulley (pulley.com)

PROMPTS

1. Determine the need to incorporate.
2. Research the best setup for your business to become incorporated, including location and entity type.
3. Find referrals to a variety of potential lawyers who would be a good fit for your business.

4. Discuss equity distribution as a team for the initial share issuance.

5. Evaluate online services that can help you incorporate your business.

6. Source the legal documents you will need to:
   - Incorporate the business
   - Close a round of funding
   - Sign your first customer
   - Hire your first employee

WORKBOOK

Get the Startup Tactics Legal Workbook, which will help you map out your legal needs, identify the best representation for your business, determine steps to incorporation, align on equity distribution, and document the organization. Within you will find worksheets that include:

1. Need and Timing: Determine your need to incorporate and introduce legal documentation.
2. Representation: Evaluate a variety of legal service providers to identify the best option.
3. Incorporation: Identify the best path forward to incorporate.
4. Equity: Establish the equity breakdown for each of the current members of the team.
5. Documentation: Secure the documentation you will need to conduct business.

ADDITIONAL RESOURCES

→ **Get the Workbook!** Visit StartupTactics.net/legal

Finance

Path to Greatness—Building the Financial Model and Setting Up the Piggy Bank

12 | FINANCE

Entrepreneurs must convince others—and, more importantly, themselves—that they can create a business that achieves significant growth in the first five years. That growth may be a reflection of revenue goals. For an innovation-driven entrepreneurial venture, for example, entrepreneurs may seek to tell a story of how they will grow to $50M in revenue by year five.

To achieve such significant growth, an upfront investment—often referred to as innovation and product development debt—will be needed. The first step in fundraising is determining how much money you want to raise in each round. Your financial plan is a key element in making that determination because it provides an estimated projection of revenues and expenses rooted in the assumptions from your business plan. These assumptions will be based on work you have done while setting your foundations and goals, testing the market, and developing the early product.

In This Tactic, You Will:

- Explore the differences between startup finance and corporate finance.
- Build a financial model that includes your revenue plan, expenses, and staffing plan.
- Explore the assumptions that serve as inputs to your financial model.
- Set up a bank account for your business.

Startup Finance versus Corporate Finance

Startup finance is quite different from finance in a large, established organization. The key goals for finance remain the same: predict future finances, measure financial performance, and communicate this information to stakeholders. These stakeholders include investors, board members, advisors, employees, partners, and, in some cases, customers as well. Beyond that, however, things differ in a few key ways.

First, the finances are rooted mostly in assumptions rather than in historical data. New ventures do not have years and years of historical data to support forward-looking financial projections.

Second, the inputs to a financial plan for a new innovation-driven venture must demonstrate more scalable growth and the levers that make that happen are much different. For example, unlike a large, corporate organization that leverages M&A for growth, a new venture in the early days will leverage its performance and key metrics to drive growth.

And third, the sources of funds for a new venture are much different than those of an established organization. Unlike a large corporation that can leverage the public market and issue bonds, a new venture must rely on other forms of capital. We will explore sources of funding in more detail in Tactic 14, Fundraising.

There are far more unknowns in startup finance, which means more uncertainty and risk. Using the inputs from the business planning process and hard data from earlier tactics as inputs to your financial plan will allow you to manage the uncertainty and develop a financial plan that best reflects future potential reality.

Basic Startup Financial Literacy

When you're a startup CEO, your number one job is not to run out of money. To ensure you can continue to run the business and make payroll for your employees, you must develop a financial plan that predicts what will happen and measures your performance. This plan will most likely manifest as a "hockey stick" graph. Every new venture has a hockey stick graph that shows a slow start before experiencing exponential growth.

Since all new ventures present that same hockey stick graph, it's your job to make sure you can explain the believable assumptions you used to arrive at your own particular hockey stick growth predictions. This process involves estimating your revenue plan, product-related expenses, staffing, and organization expenses. While your venture will ideally exist for far longer, you can begin the process with a five-year financial plan.

Revenue Plan

The financial planning process begins with a revenue plan. Revenue is the amount of money received or brought into the business, mainly from customers. For each month or quarter over the next five years, estimate the number of customers you will have, how many products they will buy from you (including both your first product and future products you will release in future years), what they will pay for those products, and any other associated services they may purchase. After building a rough revenue plan, check your work, focusing first on whether the plan is realistic.

The most frequent thing I encounter that requires revision is the projected number of customers in the first month or quarter. These predictions are often unrealistic and put the business behind the plan right out of the gate unnecessarily.

When entrepreneurs building B2B businesses show that they will have 25 customers in the first quarter of their financial plan, I ask them to consider whether that is in fact possible. I ask, "Can you say with confidence you will have signed contracts and incoming wires confirmed from 25 businesses in three months given that you have a nine-month sales cycle?" The 25 number is quickly revised to a more believable zero, with a few customers planned for quarters two and three.

For each of the customers you believe you will have in the first month or quarter, confirm that you know who they are. You should know them, have spoken to them, validated their interest, and confirmed that they fit the demographics and psychographics of your next 10 customers. You should also ask yourself how closely they match your persona.

As entrepreneurs, we like to think we can achieve greatness. We can, but we must also be realistic. Not just for investors, who will poke holes in our financial models, but for ourselves.

DISCIPLINED ENTREPRENEURSHIP

REFER TO STEP

5

BEACHHEAD PERSONA

REFER TO STEP

9

FIRST 10 CUSTOMERS

Your revenue numbers in the financial plan should tie back to your organization-level goals from Tactic 1 and to your sales pipeline from Tactic 6. Leveraging the work from the business planning process and application of the tactics makes the financial modeling process simpler and ultimately ensures that your financial plan can be justified.

Cost of Goods Sold

Based on your revenue plan, you know how many units of each of your products you expect to sell. With these estimates, you can predict the expense you will incur to produce each of the products. The cost of goods sold (COGS) is calculated based on all expenses incurred to produce each additional unit. This includes materials, labor, and overhead directly attributed to each unit. Typically this would include parts for manufacturing, costs to warehouse and ship a unit of product, and the people-hours associated with manufacturing the product. The COGS includes the costs incurred to create the product, but not the costs related to marketing and sales to sell the product, nor the upfront costs for manufacturing, such as tooling and assembly line buildouts.

In a venture selling a hardware product, the COGS are straightforward and there's usually a lower margin, meaning that the amount of profit (revenue minus expenses) is lower per unit. In a software business, this is much different because the expense incurred to produce an additional unit is significantly lower.

For software, there is no manufacturing facility per se and there are no physical parts. Instead, the software already developed can simply be offered to customers over the internet. For software-based ventures, salaries for engineers who develop the software are not included in the costs of goods sold, unlike the factory workers who would build physical products. In software-based ventures, the software is not developed on a per-customer basis—unless work is through a consulting model. Instead, software development is an upfront research and development (R&D) expense included elsewhere in your financial model. If your business offers the option to purchase additional product-related services outlined in the revenue plan, you can include the expense incurred for staff to provide the service and support customers.

Staffing

In addition to unit-based COGS related to your revenue plan, your venture needs a team not just to build the product but also to build the business. To build out the staffing section of your financial model, list all the roles you must fill over the next five years. Since not all roles need filling on day 0, for each role decide when you will need to make that hire and when you might need additional individuals in that role. For example, you will need one chief technology officer and you may choose to hire them sooner rather than later, as discussed in Tactic 10, Engineering.

However, you may need nine engineers, with one hired in three months, another hired in six months, and three more hired 12 months out, bringing on the rest during the following few years.

Next you need a plan for how much each of these individuals will make. Determine estimated average cash salaries for each role and be sure to add in benefits. Far too many early startup financial models incorporate cash salaries yet overlook the expense of benefits, but you can safely estimate those will cost an additional 30% on top of the cash salary for each employee. Also estimate a cost of living adjustment (COLA) for each individual on the team, which fluctuates but can be ballparked at 3% per year.

You can see that the expense is not just salaries—it all adds up. But people are the most important element of your business and it's worth it!

Operating Expenses

With your staffing plan in place—which will account for a significant portion of your overall expenses—you must estimate other operating expenses. These will span three key buckets: research and development (R&D), marketing and sales (M&S), and general and administrative (G&A).

Your R&D expenses will include all salaries and benefits from your staffing plan as well as technology supplies, such as computers and hardware prototyping supplies, not related to the direct production of each additional unit of product. Your M&S expenses include everything you previously calculated using Tactic 5, Marketing, into your cost of customer acquisition (COCA), such as travel, PR, trade shows, advertising campaigns, and the like. And finally, your G&A expenses include salaries for other individuals—including the CEO—as well as legal expenses, office space (if that's an operating expense, such as rent, as opposed to capital expenses, as outlined in the next section), telephone and internet access, and other spending related to the ongoing operation of the business.

DISCIPLINED ENTREPRENEURSHIP

REFER TO STEP

19

COST OF CUSTOMER ACQUISITION

Capital Expenses

Unlike operating expenses, capital expenses include major purchases that will be used by the business over the long term. The simplest example applicable to early-stage ventures would be those of workstations, laptops, and monitors. For ventures that produce hardware and own their own manufacturing expenses related to the assembly line, machinery would also be included. For some businesses, especially those commercializing deep tech research, there may be other capital expenditures such as machinery used for research. In most cases, an early-stage venture will opt to conserve cash in favor of operating expenses over capital expenses.

Other Financial Inputs

Your financial plan will also include other estimates outside of revenue and expenses. These include accounts receivable, which represent the money owed to your company by customers for products or services you have already invoiced for. In a new venture, you want to reduce accounts receivable because it's better to have cash now rather than cash later. You can put those funds to work!

Similar to accounts receivable, you also need an estimate of accounts payable, or money owed by your company to suppliers for goods or services you have already been invoiced for. Again, having cash now is better than paying cash now, so leverage net terms to extend the runway of your venture. If you are building a hardware-based venture, take into account inventory expenses for any products you hold on hand.

Financial Model Outputs

The inputs to your financial model are largely assumptions from the work already completed when building your business plan and applying the previous tactics. I highly recommend beginning building your financial model by listing your assumptions in a scratchpad spreadsheet. You can leverage financial modeling templates—which will surely need to be customized—to generate the outputs you'll need. The outputs should include a balance sheet, cash flow forecast, profit and loss statement, and a graph plotting revenue and cash flow over the next five years.

When reviewing your balance sheet, you will find that your ending balance—or the amount of money you have at the end of any given period—will be negative at first. This is to be expected because—in an innovation-driven enterprise—you will have upfront innovation and product development debt. This negative bank balance comes back to your number one job as a startup CEO, which as you'll recall is to make sure you never run out of money.

Using the information from your estimated future ending balances, you can estimate the amount of funding you will need to secure an adequate runway—or the amount of time you can continue operating the business without running out of money—to keep the business operating for the next 12–18 months. We will explore how to secure the funding needed in more detail in Tactic 14, Fundraising. The expense line items included in your cash flow help you understand your burn rate—or the amount of money you spend each month—so you can clearly communicate your runway.

Path to Profitability

The other output of your financial model will be your hockey stick growth graph. This graph should be the visual asset you leverage to tell a story of how you will go from a new venture to a business that scales. At some point—ideally, roughly in year three or four for most innovation-driven startups—the business should become cash-flow positive—a point in time when the amount of cash the business brings in is greater than the amount it spends. When a business becomes cash-flow positive it has achieved "ramen profitability." Popularized by Paul Graham—co-founder of YCombinator—ramen profitability is when, as he describes, "a startup makes just enough to pay the founders' living expenses."[1] This is a major milestone for any business and buys you time as a founder. Your job becomes scaling the business operations sustainably.

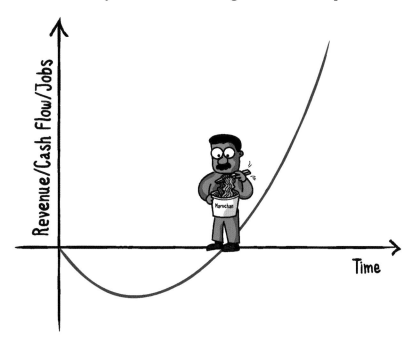

If you are building an innovation-driven enterprise you need to tell a story of how you will grow your business into one generating at least $50 million in revenue in year five. This timeline may be extended for businesses operating in some industries such as healthcare or commercializing hard technology. If you can't demonstrate a path to generating $50 million in revenue in

---

[1] http://www.paulgraham.com/ramenprofitable.html

year five you should ask yourself whether this problem is big enough to be worth the investment and effort. You may also be building an SME or lifestyle business, in which case $50M might not make sense; you may target revenue goals that are significantly lower. This is not because you are looking exclusively for profit, but rather because the amount of revenue you can generate in some ways reflects on the impact your business is making. Assuming strong margins, it is also a reflection of cash on hand that you can use to expand your impact. Coming back to the key definition of entrepreneurship—to create and capture value so that you can do so sustainably in the long term—you should be seeking to have an outsized impact, not just to profiteer.

Beyond Modeling: Ongoing Monitoring with Finance Tools

As you move forward in building the business you will need to routinely refer back to your financial model using ongoing data to revise the model. Continuing to iterate on your financial model and projections will help you measure your financial status and ultimately give you the confidence that you won't run out of money. For your model to remain up-to-date and accurate, you will need some basic accounting setup.

In the early days, you will have limited transactions and a spreadsheet might suffice for monitoring financial transactions and status. I even filed taxes in the first year for one of my startups with a simple spreadsheet. However, as you advance and the number of transactions increase—including those related to revenue and expenses—you will likely need to upgrade your tooling from Tactic 2, Systems. When the need arises, you can look for these such as QuickBooks, which will help organize your financial record keeping.

Banking

You will also need to secure a business bank account. It is important to keep all business finances separate from your personal finances for tax purposes and to increase the accuracy of your monitoring of the venture's financial status. Most consumer banks will also provide business bank accounts and you will also find some financial institutions or FinTech providers that cater to serving new ventures. To protect the future of the business—especially given the limited runway—you may choose to diversify your banking relationships by storing funds across several financial institutions.

Summary

In order to build your business you need to understand what your financial model looks like and the assumptions that will go into it. Building a comprehensive financial model includes a revenue plan, expenses, and staffing plan. This financial model should tell a story that clearly communicates how you can grow the business to be profitable and self-sustaining on a path to exponential growth. It's your responsibility as the entrepreneurial leader to understand the finances because the CEO's number one job is to make sure you never run out of money.

TOOLS OF THE TRADE

Modeling

Microsoft Excel (microsoft.com/en-us/microsoft-365/excel)

Google Sheets (google.com/sheets/about/)

Francis (francis.app)

Record Keeping

QuickBooks (quickbooks.intuit.com)

Xero (xero.com)

Zoho Books (zoho.com/us/books/)

Quicken (quicken.com)

Sage (sage.com)

NetSuite (netsuite.com/portal/products/erp/financial-management/finance-accounting.shtml)

Banking

Bank of America (bankofamerica.com/smallbusiness/)

Chase (chase.com/business)

Citizens Bank (citizensbank.com)

US Bank (usbank.com/business-banking)

Grasshopper (grasshopper.bank/)

Mercury (mercury.com)

Brex (brex.com/product/business-account)

Novo (novo.co)

Payments

Bill.com (bill.com)

Stripe (stripe.com)

Braintree (braintreepayments.com)

Adyen (adyen.com)

PROMPTS

1. Build out your financial model, including plans for revenue, costs of goods sold, staffing plan, and other operational expenses.

2. Create a bear, bull, and base case of your financial model outlining the possible outcomes with different inputs over time.

3. Review your model with someone outside of your team to get feedback.

4. Explore different startup-friendly banking options.

5. Sign up for a payments processor so you're ready to collect your first payment.

WORKBOOK

Get the Startup Tactics Finance Workbook, which will help you map your revenue plan, expenses, staffing needs, and operational expenses. The workbook will prepare you with a full financial model for the first few years of your business.

ADDITIONAL RESOURCES

→ **Get the Workbook!** Visit StartupTactics.net/finance

Pitch Deck Design
Pitch Decks for Startups

After completing your financial plan, it's time to tackle the next asset you will need for fundraising: the pitch deck. Having a strong business plan is not good enough—you must be able to effectively communicate that plan to others to acquire the resources you need.

The startup pitch deck is more art than science and serves as a teaser or gut check to warrant further questions.

Developing the pitch deck for a new startup is not an exercise of checking boxes. That's not to say that the visual design is the most important, but rather that you must include more than just the appropriate information. You need to tell a clear, concise, compelling story.

In This Tactic, You Will:

- Tell your venture's story: one that doesn't just communicate information but that gives your audience goosebumps.
- Create a pitch deck for your new venture.
- Practice your public speaking skills.

Audience Identification

The first step to developing your pitch deck is identifying your audience. It's likely that you will have pitch decks for a variety of audiences and content *can* be reused. However, you should start with the goal of acquiring additional resources, specifically for fundraising. To define your audience, first identify which individuals will see your pitch deck and who they might share it with.

Then determine why your audience cares. You can do so by identifying their incentives, which helps you understand what to include. For example, a venture capitalist looking at your deck is incentivized by financial returns from de-risked investments. Therefore you know for that audience you must zero in on the need to de-risk as much as possible in the deck.

Finally, identify what you want from your audience. What is your ask of them? Keep in mind that while you might have an end goal in your engagement with the audience, your ask should be the next step. For example, with an audience of potential customers, you may want them to sign up for a subscription but, in the short term with this pitch deck, the ask may be to simply join your waitlist. Likewise, with an audience of venture capitalists, you may want them to write a $1M check, but your short-term ask is simply for a follow-up meeting.

You will see an example at the end of this tactic where an entrepreneur needs to present to a large audience. Before you prepare your story and slides, you should consider not just the specifics of the audience but also the size of the audience. You may be pitching to one person in a conversation, several people in a meeting, a roomful of individuals, or thousands of people either in person or online.

Story Over Slides

Most entrepreneurs begin by designing a slide deck or laying out information on a canvas. I ask you to take a step back and remember that the members of your audience are humans, and humans live to be entertained. Although you are not putting on a theatrical performance—nor should you—there is value in thinking about your pitch deck from the perspective of an entertainer. Entertainment writers think regularly about the emotions they wish to extract from their audience. You can apply the same lens of looking to extract emotions from your audience. Start by designing the story you will tell and then translate that story into slides.

I think back often to a pitch delivered by Dr. Ryan Gillis of Thiozen. Gillis initially began pitching his business with a slide-first approach. In the further development of his pitch for Thiozen, he used a story-first approach and began the pitch with a sad statement: "California is burning."[1] This was not a happy statement, but it set the stage and raised the stakes and was the beginning of a story that culminated with the introduction of their solution to addressing climate change.

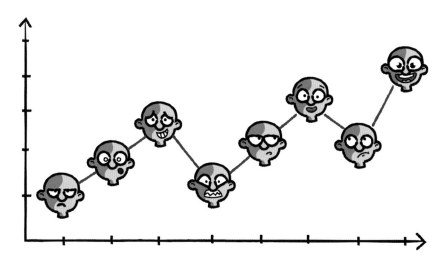

Tactically, this may require getting some sticky notes. On each sticky note, include one part of the story with a topic, key point, and most importantly, the emotion you intend to elicit from your audience. You can arrange these sticky notes in a logical, narrative order for your story. By rearranging the order, you can evoke emotions that align with one of the six emotional arcs of stories extracted from an analysis of 1,327 stories from Project Gutenberg through a research study

---

[1] https://vimeo.com/459091479

outlined in an article named "The emotional arcs of stories are dominated by six basic shapes."[2] Conducted by a team led by Andrew J Reagan, the research found support for six emotional arcs:

- "Rags to riches" (rise)
- "Tragedy" or "Riches to rags" (fall)
- "Man in a hole" (fall-rise)
- "Icarus" (rise-fall)
- "Cinderella" (rise-fall-rise)
- "Oedipus" (fall-rise-fall)

Identify which of the above types of stories you're trying to tell and use that as an input to your storyline. In most cases, you will want to end with a high degree of happiness in your storyline since it is a pitch.

For each component of your story, try using one sticky note. Then organize the sticky notes according to the emotion you want your audience to feel. In the example seen here, notice that the story arc you see from the alignment of the sticky notes both starts and ends on high notes:

Entrepreneurs can plan their storyline by using sticky notes. Each sticky note should have the topic, key point, and the emotion that they want their audience to feel. Then, the sticky notes can be arranged from start to finish of the story following the intended emotion arc.

Using sticky notes allows you to rearrange and revise the components of your story to craft the most compelling arc.

---

[2] https://epjdatascience.springeropen.com/articles/10.1140/epjds/s13688-016-0093-1

Why would we want to rearrange? While the core components should all be covered in every entrepreneur's investment pitch, the order shouldn't be consistent. For example, a recent delta v team of MIT undergraduates starting a quantum computing platform business included their team early on in their story. This allowed them to gain early credibility with and conviction from their audience since their team included industry thought leaders who have written 50 research publications and been quoted 2,000 times. Other ventures might include the team later in the story, choosing to focus on the problem, solution, and market prior.

After aligning on the story you wish to tell, you can begin designing simple visual slides to communicate your key points.

Revisions

Now that you've crafted your story, you must be ready to close the deal, right? Not just yet. There are a few reasons why you would change your story.

Every investor you pitch is unique and deserves a customized story crafted to meet their interests and investment thesis. Now that you have your core story comprising the crucial components, you can modify it to meet your needs for each presentation you give. You might consider an investor's portfolio, their investment thesis, or specific asks you have of each investor you pitch, working those into your story so it is tailored for them.

You should also be gathering feedback from every meeting you get based on the line of questions, push-back on specific portions of your story, and also what's working well. If you take notes after each meeting, you can look at a week's worth of meetings holistically to identify patterns that emerge from multiple investors. As you hear repeated questions, work to proactively address these in your story.

Don't think of your story and your pitch as a finished product, but rather a continuously changing pitch that will continue improving.

Slide Design

Now that you've developed and revised your story for your proper audience, it is time to begin designing slides, be careful not to overdevelop the deck. Consider what the venue for the deck will be. You should have one version that is a live presentation pitch deck and another that is an asynchronous deck.

Your in-person pitch deck might be delivered in a live, in-person or virtual meeting where you want to make sure that your audience is focused on you, not the slides. The 10/20/30 rule—popularized by famous entrepreneur and marketing expert Guy Kawasaki—states that you should have no more than 10 slides, talk no longer than 20 minutes, and use at least a 30-point font size. The exact number of slides may vary depending on your presentation style and the amount of time you have for the meeting. The 30-point font size rule should always hold true for live presentation decks regardless of the duration. For these pitches, prioritize visual slides with not much more than one line of text.

Your asynchronous deck is used to communicate information about your venture via email rather than in a real-time presentation setting. This deck can contain much more information that provides the audience with the context they won't get from your voice. Keep in mind that an emailed deck can be shared with others whom you wouldn't necessarily want to have access.

Looking for the best of both worlds? Consider an asynchronous pitch deck that is recorded using your video and voice overlaid on the deck!

ADDITIONAL RESOURCES

→ **Share Your Deck!** Upload a copy of your pitch deck: StartupTactics.net/share

---

Critical Components

While you need to tell a compelling story and not just check the boxes, your audience is looking for key information. While each audience will have specific needs, use this list as a starting point:

- Introduction: Who are you?
- Target Customer and Problem: Who are you helping? What problem are you solving?
- Market: How big are the Beachhead Market and overall markets? What market forces make now the right time for the venture?
- Solution/Product: How are you solving the problem?
- Moat and Core: How can you address the problem in a way that others can't?
- Competition: What other solutions or alternatives exist on the market?
- Team: Who is on the team and why are you uniquely qualified to solve the problem?
- Traction: How much traction have you made to date? *Include data from previous tactics!*
- Business Model: How do you make money?
- Financials: How does this become a big business? *No spreadsheets—only a graph!*
- Plan: What are your next steps?
- Key Points and Ask: What three things do you want your audience to remember? What do you want immediately from your audience?

These components should serve as a starting point of boxes you need to check, but investor pitches are not one-size-fits-all. Every business has unique requirements that must be pitched, and different investors or sources of funding may need additional points addressed.

Be sure to cover these key slides, but it can be helpful to have backup slides to provide visuals to complement your answers to audience questions when possible. Some backup slides to consider for your appendix include:

- Technology: What is the core technology and how does it work?
- Intellectual Property: What protection do you have for your inventions?
- Use Case: How does the target customer actually use the product from end to end?
- Team-Plus: What do your future hiring plans look like?
- Product Roadmap: Where does the product go from here? What is the product vision?
- Detailed Finances: What are the inputs to the hockey stick graph?

Tips and Tricks

Presenting your pitch deck is mostly an art and one you can master. Here are a few tips and tricks as you proceed with the development and delivery of your pitch deck and that can take your public speaking skills to the next level:

- **Practice makes perfect.** To master the presentation of your pitch deck you will need to practice over and over. This includes with your audience and also with co-founders, advisors, other entrepreneurs, and even yourself. Try recording yourself delivering your pitch deck presentation and then watch it to provide yourself with feedback.
- **Practice out loud.** You won't deliver your pitch deck presentation silently. If you practice that way, the delivery will not be as strong. When you practice, best prepare yourself to deliver your presentation by practicing out loud.
- **Your enthusiasm is critical.** If you are not enthusiastic about your business, nobody else will be either. Ensure your enthusiasm shines through in the presentation of your pitch deck.
- **You are building this business.** With so many unknowns, pitch deck presentations often include phrases such as "We will do x, y, and z," or "We plan to do x, y, and z." If you are building this business then make sure people know it! Instead, use phrases such as "We are building x, y, and z" or "We are x, y, and z."

- **Leave your audience with three key points.** People can reasonably remember three things. What are the three things you want your audience to remember next Tuesday when they are eating lunch with a friend or colleague?

- **Simplify!** Less is more and you're better off running short than trying to cram more information into your pitch deck presentation than there is reasonable time for.

- **End with your ask.** Don't be afraid to ask a question at the very end and wait for a response. It's okay to put your audience on the spot when there is something you need from them.

EXAMPLE

Amira Health

Loewen Cavill, MIT Mechanical Engineering '20, is the co-founder and CEO of Amira, formerly known as AuraBlue, which developed a wearable device to predict and preemptively counteract hot flashes. The device is a bracelet that monitors users while they sleep, anticipates a hot flash, and then works to cool the user down before the hot flash happens.

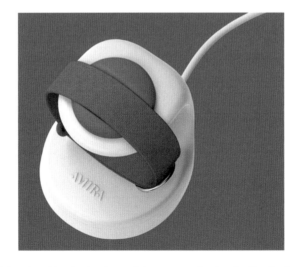

When a hot flash begins, the Amira bracelet communicates to the Amira cooling system.

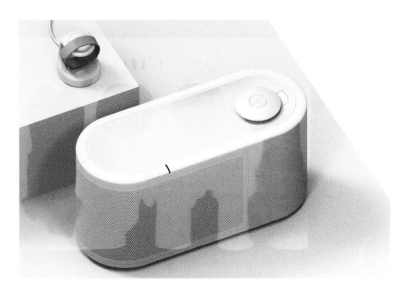

The cooling system receives a notification from the bracelet when a hot flash begins and activates the under-sheet cooling mattress pad.

Cavill and her team of mechanical engineers and computer scientists participated in the MIT delta v startup accelerator and concluded the program with a pitch of their business to thousands of people online. In preparing for their Demo Day, Cavill mastered the content and delivery of her pitch.

The pitch centers around the story of Cavill's aunt, Aunt Kate, who suffered from hot flashes and had been looking for a solution. The story Cavill tells about her aunt hooks you in as a listener and keeps you with her as she presents the business. Despite being a team of engineers, nowhere do they overload the audience with technical details, just the fact that they have an amazing business.

The pitch deck at Demo Day helped bring in inbound investors, beta users, and hires all in one. Subsequent pitch decks used specifically for fundraising pitches to venture capitalists employed the same storytelling tactics you'll see in their Demo Day pitch and led to their $3M round.

ADDITIONAL RESOURCES

→ **Watch the Pitch!** Watch the pitch video and see the slides by visiting StartupTactics.net/pitch-deck/amira

The MIT delta v Demo Day presentation delivered by Cavill is an excellent example of a high-quality pitch presentation for a broad audience.

Summary

Your pitch deck will be the asset that you use to acquire additional resources, including raising money from investors and recruiting new talent. It is important that you communicate in a manner to which people will react: a story. Before creating a slide deck you should start with crafting a compelling story. Designed intentionally, the story can then be translated into a presentation. You should consider two presentations: one to email with a goal of getting a meeting that contains more information and another for in-person presentations that you can speak to. What story would you want to hear about your business?

ADDITIONAL RESOURCES

→ **Learn More About Public Speaking!** Visit StartupTactics.net/public-speaking to explore how you can improve your public speaking skills.

TOOLS OF THE TRADE

Storytelling

Post-It Notes (amazon.com/Sticky-Notes-Bright-Colored-Super/dp/B07DMZVC5M)

Miro (miro.com)

FigJam (figma.com/figjam/)

Lucid Spark (lucidspark.com)

Mural (mural.co)

Whimsical (whimsical.com)

Presentation Software

Google Slides (slides.google.com)

Microsoft PowerPoint (microsoft.com/en-us/microsoft-365/powerpoint)

Beautiful.ai (beautiful.ai)

Pitch.com (pitch.com)

Prezi (prezi.com)

PitchDeck (pitchdeck.io)

PROMPTS

1. Determine the different audiences to whom you will need to present a pitch deck.
2. Align on the purpose and call to action for your pitch deck.
3. Craft your storyline for your new pitch deck using sticky notes.
4. Share your storyline with a friendly audience for feedback.
5. Source high-quality visuals from the internet for your slides.
6. Turn your storyline into a compelling slide deck you can share with others.
7. Refine based on feedback from your friendly audience.

WORKBOOK

Get the Startup Tactics Pitch Deck Workbook, which will help you craft a storyline, outline the content for your pitch deck, and source design assets. Within you will find worksheets that include:

1. Purpose: Begin with the purpose of your deck and who you are targeting.
2. Themes and Emotions: Designing for emotional extraction improves the story.
3. Story Arc: Modeling your approach after movies, you can arrange themes to tell the best story.
4. Content: With the story arc designed, identify content for each slide.
5. Design: Make it easy by creating a high-quality design with a template.
6. Appendix: Identify and create relevant backup slides for your appendix.

ADDITIONAL RESOURCES

➜ **Get the Workbook!** Visit StartupTactics.net/pitch-deck

Fundraising

Executing Your Venture's Fundraising Plan

14 FUNDRAISING

Whathat's more important than planning to fundraise? Actually doing it. Entrepreneurs must sustain their momentum to continue demonstrating growth throughout the fundraising process.

Fundraising can augment one of your two most precious resources: money. (The other is time, discussed in the next chapter.) Fundraising is a full-time job that takes you away from building your business. Running the fundraising processes efficiently will be incredibly important so that you can get back to doing what you do best as an entrepreneur.

In This Tactic, You Will:

- Set the milestones for each round of funding that you will seek to secure.
- Determine the best fit source of funding—it might not be the most obvious.
- Design your fundraising sales process based on the source of funding you select.
- Build a lead list of highly targeted potential investors specific to your business.
- Get introductions to those investors identified on your lead list.

Milestone-Based Financing

pre-seed   seed   series A   series B

Rather than raise as much money as you can convince investors to give you, you can and should reduce the investment risk by adopting a milestone-based financing approach. This not only reduces risk for investors and the venture but also maximizes value for you as a founder. The more money you take earlier in the venture's lifecycle, the more equity you give up, which reduces the amount of time you will have to make an impact or reach an exit such as an IPO, acquisition, or merger. Rather than raise capital to fund the business operations for the next five years upfront or achieve a larger, more elusive breakthrough, you can raise money in multiple rounds. A typical sequence is friends and family, pre-seed, seed, Series A, Series B, Series C, and so on. Milestones must be hit to convince investors that your venture is worthy of more money each round.

There are two primary types of milestones: business milestones and technical milestones. In most cases, business milestones will be the primary drivers of fundraising. This varies only based on the type of risk associated with the success of a business.

When a venture has greater market risk than technical risk, then the business milestones will take priority. However, when technical risk outweighs market risk—in hard tech or deep tech, for example— technical milestones may take priority.

In ventures with primarily market risk—when there's a reasonable assumption that the technology *can* be brought to life—business milestones such as a waitlist in the early stages or a certain amount of annual recurring revenue (ARR) will unlock the next round of funding. This next round most often supports hitting a technical milestone, which subsequently leads to furthering the venture's business milestones.

When the opposite is true and there is more technology risk than market risk—a topic I have explored in detail in conversations with Murat Onen, PhD in electrical engineering and computer science from MIT and the founder and CEO of Eva—the focus should be on proving out technical milestones. Unlocking technical milestones when technical risk is greater than market risk will unlock funding to ultimately get to market. Onen is building 100 times higher performance analog AI training solutions to replace energy-hungry graphic processing units (GPUs) and to enable sustainable large-scale training model development. Given the very high demand for AI compute, a solution in this space is expected to see very little to no market risk. On the other hand, Eva's technology is deeply rooted in applied physics and mathematics, and thus will likely require multiple years of development before achieving paying customers. Innovations like Onen's tend to have a greater potential impact but also introduce additional risk for the entrepreneur. Because there is an extended amount of time between founding and becoming cash-flow positive, more equity capital is required, which can dilute the founder, and more time is needed, during which external forces can change. A technology that requires ten years of development, (e.g., fusion power) can face many external factors during that time—a lot can happen in 10 years.

Regardless of your venture's balance between technical and market risk, in preparation for the fundraising process, find alignment between your organization-level goals from Tactic 1 and the financial plan developed in Tactic 12. These goals and projections enable you to define your month-by-month reasonable and achievable business or technical milestones. These goals and your milestones extend beyond your beachhead market as you chart the course towards follow-on markets.

Your fundraising milestones will be the key inputs to how you communicate your progress to potential funders. These milestones facilitate communicating: 1) what you said you were going to do, 2) what you achieved, and 3) what you plan to do next.

DISCIPLINED
ENTREPRENEURSHIP

REFER TO STEP

2

BEACHHEAD
MARKET

REFER TO STEP

14

TAM FOR FOLLOW
ON MARKETS

Sources of Funding

Entrepreneurs are trained, formally and informally, to believe they must raise venture capital. News articles always hype up startups and entrepreneurs who have raised significant amounts of money or reached unicorn status. However, venture capital is *not* a fit for every new venture, particularly in its earliest stages.

In venture capital, each fund has limited partners who invest in a pool. They are looking for significant returns across the portfolio, but only on a fraction of the fund's investments. That means for each deal they look at, they must see a path to a 50 times return or more so that they can increase the odds that their fund—which sees most investments produce little to no return—produces a sizable overall return. If your venture is unlikely to return a 50-times-plus return, then venture capital might not be your most appropriate funding source.

Luckily, there are a variety of other sources available. A systematic analysis of the best fit for your venture can help you save time and maximize ownership of your business:

Type of Funding	Dilution	Considerations	Source(s)
Your profits	Nondilutive	No debt	Customers
Grants		No debt, may have strings	Government, foundations
Donations		No debt, may have strings	Crowdfunding, Kickstarter
Recoverable grant		Paid back if things go well	Social investor, donors
Profit sharing		Giving up a % of profits	Suppliers, partners
Debt/Loans		Must be paid back	Banks, private firms
Convertible debt (convertible note) or SAFE	Dilutive	Converts to equity in future	Friends and family, angel investors, venture capitalists
Equity		Giving up % of ownership	Angel investors, venture capitalists

Scott Maxwell, the founder of OpenView Venture Partners, said the best venture capitalists for your business are your own customers.[1] Your profits are always the best source of funding because you can continue selling to customers, learning from them, and developing the business to generate more profits.

By funding your business with your own profits, you will have the opportunity to refine your customer segment, focus on high-quality customers, and lower costs, all on your timeline rather than that of an investor or a bank. Most importantly, you maintain ownership of your business because your own profits are nondilutive.

---

[1] https://www.pehub.com/scott-maxwell-the-1-vc-in-the-world-your-customers/

It is, however, difficult to bootstrap and self-fund your venture until you reach profitability, and even then your relatively meager coffers may limit your growth potential because of the innovation and product development debt required to build a scalable innovation-driven enterprise on a shoestring budget.

Running a Fundraising Process

Now that you understand the different funding sources, such as equity, debt, and customer funding, let's work through the steps to source money from them. Think of it similarly to the sales process you might use when selling to early customers that we explored in Tactic 6.

Regardless of your funding source, the fundraising process is very similar to the sales decision-making process, so you will need a funnel. You will have funding leads, prospects, qualified investors, and so on. The major difference is that the process to close a deal involves different activities. The pipeline may look different for different sources of funding. There is a typical process for venture deals, for instance, that is different from the process used in applying for grants. For this example, we'll focus on venture funding, which typically follows this process:

DISCIPLINED
ENTREPRENEURSHIP

REFER TO STEP

13

CUSTOMER
ACQUISITION
PROCESS

1. Intro sent
2. Phone call
3. Meeting(s)
4. Partner meeting
5. Diligence
6. Term sheet
7. Check

All of these steps should be tracked because they indicate different probabilities of closing. For example, the chances of securing funding from an investor after a first phone call are less than 10%. Multiply that by the typical check size that a source of funding provides, and now you have your expected funding from that source. The likelihood of closing on an investment increases in size for individual potential sources of funding as you progress through the fundraising pipeline. The likelihood will vary widely by firm, industry, and the specifics of the venture, but a sample is included in the chart seen here.

Stage	Likelihood of Investment
Introduction request sent	1%
Phone call with potential investor	5%
First meeting with investor	10%
Second meeting with investor	20%
Partner meeting	40%
Due diligence	60%
Term sheet	90%
Check (money in the bank)	100%

Note that the likelihood of closing the investment does not hit 100% until the investor's money hits your bank account. This can often happen in the diligence process, which is an investor's audit of the company before they decide to invest. I have seen red-lined term sheets pulled before closing. As they say, don't count your chickens before they hatch!

For example, if the probability of securing funding is 40% after a successful partner meeting during which you ask for a $300,000 investment, then your expected funds are $120,000. In isolation, this number doesn't mean much, but when combined with other funding sources you're chasing you can tell whether you are on target to raise what you need from multiple sources. This should seem similar to how we use probabilities of sales opportunities to forecast revenue.

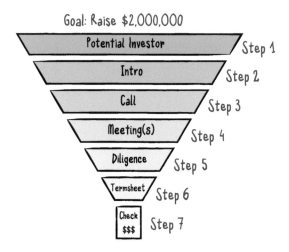

Similar to how the sales process from Tactic 6 can start with leads or potential customers, we start by generating investor leads—or potential individuals or organizations—that could invest in your company. Then, similar to how you would filter and prioritize customer leads, we will do the same with potential investors.

Building the Lead List

At this point we should have a list of groups and individuals who could be potential investors (sometimes referred to as angels). To make sure that we're able to effectively run our fundraising process we'll want to keep all of our information in one place, using a system from Tactic 2.

For each potential investor or source of funding, we'll want to have some key information:

- Fund: If the funding source is a venture capital fund or angel group, we'll want to have the name and some key information about it such as the fund size and classification (more on classifications into tiers later in the section "Prioritization: Sequencing the Leads").

- Partner/Individual: You should know which venture capital partner you are targeting or which angel is your champion. You'll also want to have their LinkedIn, a list of related investments they have made, their typical check size, the number of investments they make each year, the industries they focus on, and how you can get in front of them. You'll also want to list your running status notes covering your interactions with them.

- Progress: Last, you'll want to track where the funding source sits in your fundraising pipeline.

Armed with this information, you're ready to take your lead list of potential investors and start turning them into actual leads.

Generating Leads

Take a two-pronged approach to generating investor leads. First, figure out who you already know and leverage your existing relationships. Then identify target investors and figure out how best to get in front of them.

Who You Already Know

Depending on your time and experience in startups, venture capital, and/or with other funding sources, you may already have a network of people to tap for assistance. Start with this list, because people you already have a relationship with (hopefully) know you and your ability to execute.

This credibility is one of the most important factors in an investor's decision as they evaluate a team's ability to execute, and an existing relationship can help de-risk that factor.

To better understand who you already know, review past relationships. A good place to start is LinkedIn. You can begin by searching and filtering your first-degree connections. It might be as simple as searching that cohort for "investor." You will likely want to refine that search to be more targeted, and we'll cover details on how to do so later in this section.

Who You Need to Know

Chances are that your network doesn't comprise every good potential investor out there. When this is the case, you must identify good target investors and then figure out the best way to reach them. What makes a good target investor? Let's figure out how to identify them.

Identifying relevant investors for your business requires research. I recommend starting by looking at who is actively making investments in your industry at your stage. You can do this by conducting research in databases like Crunchbase and/or Pitchbook.

For example, if you are currently raising your seed round and looking specifically for angel groups to participate, you might run a search on Crunchbase for angel groups actively investing in seed-stage companies and making investments of under $500,000, which returns 475 results.

	Organization/Person Name	Investor Type	Description	Location	Number of Inves...	Website
Type ✕						
☐ Venture Capital	☐ Alumni Ventures	Angel Group, Micro VC	Alumni Ventures Group is a venture capital investment firm	Manchester, New Hampshi...	1,460	www.av.vc
☐ Individual/Angel	☐ Sand Hill Angels	Angel Group	Sand Hill Angels is a group of Silicon Valley angel investors	Mountain View, California, ...	719	www.sandhillangels.com
☐ Private Equity Firm	☐ Tech Coast Angels	Angel Group	Invests in high-growth start-up's headquartered in Southern	Newport Beach, California, ...	579	www.techcoastangels.com
☐ Accelerator	☐ SFC Capital	Angel Group, Micro VC	Early-stage investor combining its own angel syndicate & seed	Northwich, Cheshire, Unite...	515	www.sfccapital.com/
☑ Angel Group	☐ Ontario Centres of Excelle...	Angel Group	The Ontario Centres of Excellence invests in projects	Toronto, Ontario, Canada	434	www.oc-innovation.ca
+ MORE OPTIONS	☐ New York Angels	Angel Group	New York Angels is a professional angel organization	New York, New York, Unite...	320	www.newyorkangels.com
Investments at this Funding Stage ✕	☐ Keiretsu Forum	Angel Group, Venture Capital	Keiretsu Forum is a California-based angel group that offers	Orinda, California, United S...	319	www.keiretsuforum.com
☐ Pre-Seed	☐ Elevate Ventures	Angel Group, Government ...	Elevate Ventures nurtures and develops emerging and existing ...	Indianapolis, Indiana, Unite...	245	www.elevateventures.com
☑ Seed	☐ LetsVenture	Angel Group	Let'sVenture enables startups looking to raise money to create...	Bengaluru, Karnataka, India	243	letsventure.com
☐ Series A	☐ Mumbai Angels	Angel Group	Mumbai Angels is an angel stage investment firm.	Mumbai, Maharashtra, India	214	www.mumbaiangels.com
☐ Series B	☐ StartEngine	Angel Group	StartEngine is an equity crowdfunding platform that ...	Los Angeles, California, Uni...	213	www.startengine.com
+ MORE OPTIONS	☐ SICTIC	Angel Group, Venture Capital	Swiss ICT Investor Club (SICTIC) connects smart money...	Zürich, Zurich, Switzerland	202	www.sictic.ch/
Investment Amount ✕						
$ Enter am — $ 500,000						

While there are a lot of angel groups listed, many have very specific focuses, such as one investing exclusively in healthcare. If you're starting a FinTech company, an angel group investing strictly in healthcare isn't relevant. You'll want to further refine your search by adding a parameter to your query specifying angel groups actively investing in FinTech, which reduces the number of results from 475 to 159.

You might also further refine or complement your search by looking at other companies in a similar FinTech segment to identify their early investors. Say, for example, that you are building a business around consumer stock trading. You might look at investors in Robinhood. While there are no angel groups on Crunchbase that write checks for $500,000 that invested in Robinhood, we might instead look at individual angels, which returns seven results.

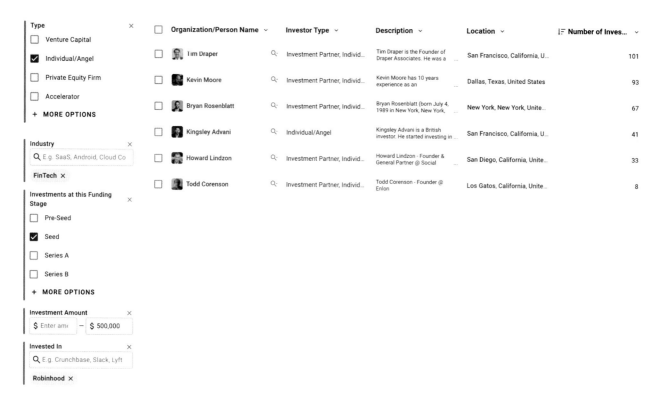

From running these search queries, we identified a number of potential investors, which we will need to keep track of. Much like a sales process, you'll want to keep these leads organized in a tracker.

A Note on Who You're Targeting

When targeting investors, especially with a focus on venture capital firms, you need to know who you're targeting. It's not just about finding the right firm; it's about finding the right individual at that firm.

First off, spending time talking to analysts or associates is not a productive use of your time. Whether outbound outreach or inbound interest, analysts and associates can't make investment decisions on behalf of their firm. That's why it is so important to identify the partner you are targeting.

Even when you have identified the partner you want to pitch at a firm, you need to ensure that they are the right partner at the firm. For example, if you're pitching your new energy startup to a partner at a firm focused on growth-stage software as a service investments, they won't invest in your venture and will likely wind up passing you off to their partner who has a focus in your industry.

Spending time pitching or building a relationship with an investor who can't or won't invest in your business can be a complete waste of time and distracting to your fundraising process.

Quality Over Quantity: Doing Your Research

You can spend countless hours fundraising, but your time is limited. Instead of taking the tempting option of meeting with any investor willing to meet with you, be selective and meet only with investors who are a fit for your business. Qualify investors to determine whether there is any possibility they could write you a check by considering public information about them, including:

- Check Size: Investors generally write a specifically sized check. For example, you wouldn't pitch an investor who only writes $5M-plus checks when you need to raise $1M total.
- Location: Some investors invest in founders building businesses in specific regions. If an investor only invests in LATAM-focused businesses or businesses based in San Francisco but you're building for a US-based market from Boston, it wouldn't make sense to waste time pitching them.
- Industry/Sector: Many investors have industry or sector-specific theses for their investments. Someone who invests exclusively in consumer mobility startups most likely won't write a check if you have an enterprise recruiting software business.

You need to identify and seek out investors who meet *all* the qualifications for your investment list. Spend time pitching only to those investors who can make an investment in your business now to conserve time.

Prioritization: Sequencing the Leads

Much like a professional baseball player wouldn't skip batting practice, you shouldn't go in cold when you're fundraising. Practice makes perfect and you wouldn't want to wind up at the plate facing a Cy Young–awarded pitcher throwing a knuckleball without some experience first. That's why I recommend properly sequencing your investor leads to get practice and prepare yourself for the most difficult questions.

Ultimately you might seek investment from a top-tier angel, venture capital firm, or other funding sources, but much like in baseball, you can hone your pitch in the minor leagues.

Firms are typically classified into tiers, with tier 1 being the top-tier firms. Before facing off with them, start with tier 2 and tier 3 firms. Doing this not only allows you to practice your pitch, but you'll also get exposure to questions in a lower-pressure setting. The questions you hear from a lot of tier 2 and tier 3 firms are a preview of what to expect from top-tier firms. This early exposure lets you prepare to answer them confidently with evidence.

Introductions: Getting in Front of Investors You've Identified

Now that you have identified potential investors, you'll need to get in front of them. What's the easiest way? Sure, you could continue down the research path, find their email address, and send them your pitch. The chances of success are pretty low when you do it that way. To maximize your odds of success, first consider all of the potential ways you can get in touch with an investor. Let's take a look at some of the options.

The best way to connect with a potential investor is through a good introduction, but not all introductions are equal. The person who introduces you can have a significant impact on your chances of success in getting a meeting. The best introduction to an investor is from a successful portfolio founder or CEO who runs a successful company the investor already invested in. This is someone the investor already has conversations with, whom they trust, and whose opinion they value. An introduction through a successful portfolio company founder/CEO has an extremely high likelihood of resulting in a call or meeting.

The next best introduction would be from a co-investor, which is another investor that the target investor has previously invested with. Again, a common theme here is that this introduction comes from someone the target investor already knows, trusts, and values.

You might also get an introduction to your target investor through other people they know, such as lawyers, accountants, or other service providers. While the investor knows these people, the likelihood of these introductions resulting in a call or meeting with your target investor drops significantly.

Finding individuals who can provide the best introduction requires a little bit more research. You need to figure out who can make an introduction for you, and one of the easiest ways to do so is to look them up on LinkedIn. If I needed an introduction to Bill, I might look him up and see if we have any mutual connections:

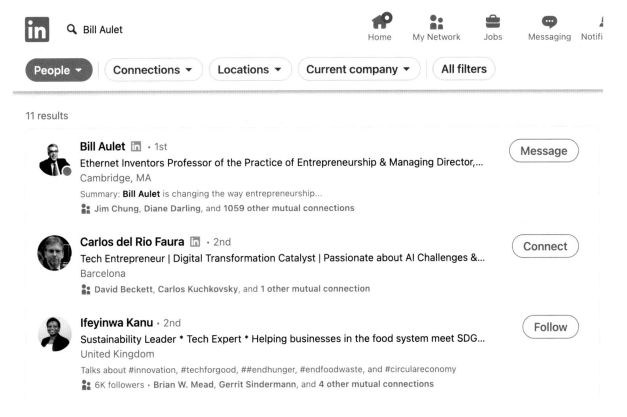

As a last resort, if you can't identify an individual you have in common, you might choose to send a cold email. These don't have a high success rate, so you should evaluate where your resources are best spent. Are you better off sending 100 cold emails, which might result in one meeting, or coordinating three good introductions from portfolio company founders, which may result in three meetings with investors? The latter is your best bet.

Requesting the Introduction

Now that you have a prioritized list of investor leads, you have to actually get the introduction. There's a good way to ask for an intro and many very bad ways. I'll take an example someone once used to ask me for introductions:

> *Hi Paul—I'm going to be in San Francisco next month and I'm trying to fill my week with investor intros. Who should I meet with while I'm there? Can you make introductions for me?*

In this example, the onus is on me to learn about the entrepreneur's business, research relevant investors for them, and write up introductions. That's a lot of work. As an entrepreneur, you should be doing this work anyway. You can enable others to make better introductions for you by including context in the introduction request that shows the thought you put into the request and the relevance of the introduction, while eliminating the need for your introducer to do any additional work. A better example of the same email might be:

> *Hi Paul,*
>
> *We're raising at ACME Inc. right now and I noticed that you're connected with Bill Aulet at MTC Investments. He led deals with a few healthcare startups in Boston like Iterative Health and DayToDay Health. Can you introduce us? I'm including a blurb describing our business below and I have attached an executive summary to this email.*
>
> *Thank you!*
>
> *[Include bullet points or brief overview of venture here]*

With this introduction request, I can simply forward it along with a note to Bill, making my job as the introducer much easier. However, when requesting an introduction, you must justify why a call or meeting is going to be worth the investor's time.

Investors receive countless introductions and requests for meetings, so they must pick and choose which they accept very carefully. For them, time is literally money. This is why you may choose to include some additional information about the new venture in your introduction request.

You wouldn't want to include your entire deck because that would give everything away; ultimately, you want the potential investor to be interested and curious for more. So a list of bullet points highlighting the most important or enticing aspects of your venture serves this purpose.

Fundraising Assets

To best prepare for your fundraising process, create a few sales assets. In addition to the live presentation and asynchronous pitch decks you prepared in Tactic 13, you should have a brief, forwardable email blurb, key bullet points about the business, and an executive summary one-pager.

Your executive summary should include the key components of your pitch deck but in a more concise, "at-a-glance" summary level. This document helps funders evaluate whether to meet with you and for them to share with their team to build excitement about your business as an investment opportunity.

Follow-up and Urgency

It is imperative to follow up with funders immediately after meeting with them. However, their life goes on and you want to make sure you remain top of mind. You can also identify something to follow up with the funder about during your meeting. It is important to take notes and identify details that you don't have with you but that you can send afterward. For example, you might share more information about the competitive landscape as a follow up if questions arise during the meeting about specific competitors and you want to demonstrate your thorough understanding of the market. Perhaps you might share a recent mention of your venture in the press or a metrics update one week after the meeting to make sure that you remain top of mind. For those funders with whom you have other mutual connections, prompt someone else to send the funder a note after your meeting.

Diligence Goes Two Ways

While you are pitching an investor, remember that you are providing them with an opportunity to invest in your venture. While they are interviewing you, in some ways you are also interviewing them.

You should find a two-way fit with your investors because you will be partners for years as the business develops.

Outside of interviewing investors during the pitch process, you can also conduct your own diligence. Begin by asking an investor for introductions to some of their portfolio company CEOs to conduct reference checks. You might also reach other portfolio company CEOs they *don't* introduce you to.

You want investors who are going to be by your side through the good times and the bad, and there will certainly be both. As you conduct diligence with other entrepreneurs, you might look to those who were not successful to get a gauge of how a potential investor will support you in the bad times.

More than Money

Investors aren't just ATMs. You want to work with funding sources that provide more than money. Scott Maxwell believes that institutional venture capital should provide meaningful value beyond the money injected into a business.[2] Added value often comes in the form of operational expertise, recruiting support, and network connections.

This is not limited to institutional capital, however. When raising convertible debt (also known as a convertible note, or in the form of a SAFE) from an angel investor, you should also be looking for the value-add. Plenty of angel investors have the cash to invest, but you should gravitate toward angels with the expertise and advisory skills that will push the business forward.

Optimizing Your Time Raising Money

Similar to your sales process, you must be disciplined when it comes to how you sell your business to investors. This process starts with sourcing: identifying potential sources of funding, getting organized to track your progress through the fundraising pipeline, sequencing your leads to set yourself up for success, and actually getting the introductions you need. With this process set up, you'll next need to prepare assets that will help you execute it, including the bullet points we mentioned for introductions and your pitch presentations.

There is far more to the tactical side of fundraising. The terminology, negotiations, and legal side of fundraising should be further explored, and I highly recommend *Venture Deals* by Brad

---

[2] https://openviewpartners.com/people/scott-maxwell/

Feld and Jason Mendelson. More specifically, you will learn more about the importance of having diligence materials ready upfront, such as your cap table, financial model, customer lists, and employment agreements (Chapter 2, "Preparing for Fundraising"). You'll also learn more in Chapter 9 about negotiation tactics, underscoring the need to do upfront research on the firm you are approaching, which will give you valuable insight into their motivations and help you navigate the conversation towards a mutually beneficial outcome.

EXAMPLE

Ecovent

Dip Patel, MIT Sloan MBA '14, was an engineer at Lockheed Martin who came up with the idea for Ecovent, which was devoted to making indoor climate control and HVAC services more intelligent. Their core product was a highly customizable climate control system managed by smartphone. Patel advanced the company and ultimately wound up continuing the development of the business in the Techstars accelerator.

Patel knew that because the business combined both software and hardware, he would need to quickly raise funding in order to finance the hardware manufacturing. He took a structured approach to fundraising that started by setting milestones for the business. By mapping business milestones, such as sales, to the amount of money that it could unlock in fundraising, Patel could estimate what technical milestones would be unlocked given their hefty price points.

Month	Business Milestone	Tech Milestone	Monthly Budget	Cumulative Budget	Pre-Money Valuation	Money Raised	Sales
1	Get Into Techstars	Design Beta System	$10,000	$50,000	$1,000,000	$600,000	
2	20 Beta Sold	Test Beta	$25,000	$75,000	$1,500,000		$100,000
3	Show Digital Marketing Traction (<$300 COCA)	Build 5 System	$50,000	$125,000	$2,000,000		
4	3 LOI's from Contractors	5 Beta Systems Working	$30,000	$155,000	$5,400,000	$2,200,000	
5	Sell ~10 Betas a Month	Show Industrial Design	$300,000	$455,000	$5,400,000		$50,000
6	Sell ~10 Betas a Month	Iterate design	$200,000	$655,000	$6,000,000		$50,000
7	Sell ~10 Betas a Month	10 Beta Systems Installed	$200,000	$855,000	$6,000,000		$50,000
8	Sell ~10 Betas a Month		$200,000	$1,055,000	$6,000,000		$50,000
9	Finalize Go to Market (B2C, Online Sales)	Finalize Design of Sensors	$250,000	$1,305,000	$6,800,000		
10	Sales Funnel / Marketing Tests - Sell More	Finalize Design of Vents	$300,000	$1,605,000	$6,800,000		
11		Fab Machined Prototypes	$300,000	$1,905,000	$6,800,000		
12		Test machined Prototypes	$250,000	$2,155,000	$6,800,000		
13	Dominate CES		$250,000	$2,405,000	$8,000,000	Intros	
14	$300K Pre-orders	Manufacturer Chosen	$200,000	$2,605,000	$9,000,000	Intros	
15	$300K Pre-orders		$200,000	$2,805,000	$9,000,000	Meetings	
16	$300K Pre-orders	Manufacturing Plan Rev 1	$250,000	$3,055,000	$9,000,000	Meetings	
17	$300K Pre-orders	UL Cert Started	$350,000	$3,405,000	$9,000,000	Diligence	
18	$300K Pre-orders	Design for Manufacturing	$500,000	$3,905,000	$15,000,000	$7,000,000	
19	$300K Pre Orders + 1 Contractor	Tooling Design 2 SKUs	$500,000	$4,405,000	$15,000,000		
20	$300K Pre-orders	Tooling Designed 14 SKUs	$2,000,000	$6,405,000	$15,000,000		
21	$300K Pre Orders + 1 Contractor	Start Production	$5,000,000	$11,405,000	$15,000,000		
22	$300K Pre Orders + 1 Contractor	Ship 200 Systems	$4,000,000	$15,405,000	$20,000,000		
23	$300K Pre Orders + 1 Contractor	Ship 200 Systems	$4,000,000	$19,405,000	$20,000,000		
24	1 Distributor Sale ($500k)	Ship 200 Systems	$4,000,000	$23,405,000	$30,000,000		
	Note: Loaded with Ecovent Example						

This fundraising plan for Ecovent outlines business milestones that need to be hit, which unlock additional funding in the "Money Raised" column. That money raised allowed the team to achieve technical milestones.

His structured approach set him up for success when communicating milestones to potential investors. He knew what he needed to accomplish to entice a potential investor, how much money he needed from them, how he would use their money, and the goals that he would work towards to advance the business with the new funding. In order to secure meetings with potential investors, he put together simple bullet points to share highlights of the business that would garner interest:

- Ecovent, spun out of MIT, Lockheed Martin, and Techstars, has developed a wireless system of vents and sensors that allow room-by-room temperature control of any building. It is the only self-configuring, fully wireless zoning system in existence. It can be installed in any building, and the system configures itself.

- The company has won Automation Product of the Year at CES, along with several MIT awards. Most recently (November 2015), Ecovent was named one of the Top 100 Inventions in *This Old House* magazine, touted as the "Holy Grail of forced-air comfort."

- The system can compensate for outdoor weather, individual temperature preferences, and inefficiencies of the building itself.

- In initial tests, Ecovent has shown savings exceeding 30%, and has identified critical home issues such as a furnace on the verge of leaking as well as mold infestations.

- Ecovent has been testing the system for over a year in beta homes, and is now in production, with a $1.5M backlog in B2C sales and $600K for the first month of B2B Sales.

- The team is in the process of raising a $5M Series A2.

You'll notice from the bullet points that Patel was raising an A2 round, or bridge round designed to provide adequate funding to reach the next set of milestones. This A2 round diverts from the initial plan he put together. It's rare that fundraising goes *exactly* to plan and Patel is the biggest proponent of having a Plan G, your course of action when plans A–F don't go the way you want.

Patel's structured approach to fundraising with alignment on his best fit source of funding, clear milestones, compelling story, and disciplined outreach led him to raise $15M, including $10M in equity to commercialize the product. His business was ultimately acquired by ConnectM in December 2016.

Summary

Fundraising is a full-time job and is a process that must be taken seriously. As an entrepreneur you have limited time and money, while investors have plenty of each. You should start by selecting the source of funding that is the best fit for your business at the current stage. Then you should build a lead list of the investors most likely to invest in your business rather than taking an approach of speaking to any investor who will speak to you. As you begin the process you will need sales assets to share, much like you would with any customer engagement. It's not an easy process, but a necessary one to fund your next milestones!

TOOLS OF THE TRADE

Research

    LinkedIn (linkedin.com)

    AngelList (angellist.com)

    Crunchbase (crunchbase.com)

    Pitchbook (pitchbook.com)

    Signal (signal.nfx.com)

PROMPTS

1. Outline business and technical milestones to identify when and how much you will need to raise during the next few years.
2. Design a storyline for raising from investors—not with slides, but with emotions.
3. Translate your storyline into an investor pitch deck.
4. Create your executive summary and intro email bullet points.
5. Identify ten potential investors (individuals, not firms!) who would be a good fit.
6. Determine the best intros you have access to and write an intro request email.

WORKBOOK

Get the Startup Tactics Fundraising Workbook, which will help you determine the best-fit source of funding, map out your fundraising milestones, create initial investor assets, and build your pipeline of investors. Within you will find worksheets that include:

1. Sources of Funding: Evaluate the best sources of funding for your new venture.
2. Milestones: Map out the business and technical milestones multiple rounds out.

3. Teasers: Develop a one-minute teaser story, introduction bullet points, and a draft email.

4. Executive Summary: Develop a one-page overview of the business opportunity.

5. Sourcing: Identify investors who you believe would be a good fit for your fundraise.

6. Intros: Craft an introduction request email that is forwardable.

7. Pipeline: Systematically track the investors you identified as good fits.

ADDITIONAL RESOURCES

→ **Get the Workbook!** Visit StartupTactics.net/fundraising

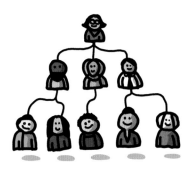

Hiring

Finding and Onboarding Your First Ten Employees

The only way for an entrepreneur to gain more of their second most precious resource—time—is by recruiting high-performing individuals. The stakes for these early hires is so important for entrepreneurs because a bad hire can actually decrease this precious resource.

After beginning the fundraising process, it's time to increase your organizational bandwidth. More time is only possible with more people. Often, founders think they can add time as a resource by burning the candle at both ends, but the venture development process is a long-term endeavor and must be treated as a marathon, not a sprint. Even so, do not hire until you have to. Even when flush with cash after a fresh round of funding, you don't have the money to waste on hiring someone you don't obviously need.

The old saying "If you want to go fast, go alone, and if you want to go far, go together" holds true when developing a new venture. While you and your co-founding team should remain lean for as long as possible, you cannot forget that you are working toward a grand vision. To achieve that grand vision you will need to go far, which requires a team.

The people you bring on board will drive your business forward and are the venture's most important assets. Each additional person you add will have a material impact on the business, so care must be taken in the recruiting and hiring process.

Be ridiculously selective of who you bring on your team. It will save you massive headaches and time down the line, which can distract you from building your business.

In This Tactic, You Will:

- Write the job description for your next hire based on the gaps in your team.
- Post your job description to popular job board websites.
- Proactively identify potential candidates through advanced searches.
- Interview candidates to determine who will be the best fit for your team.
- Create compelling compensation options for new hires.

Determining Who You Need to Hire

Because the acquisition of more time requires money—or the more costly equity compensation—you want to hire only those you need. There are two approaches to determining this.

First, start by analyzing your goals from Tactic 1, your financial plan from Tactic 12, and your fundraising milestones from Tactic 14. Each time you acquire additional resources—or lose any—you should reevaluate your goals. When determining your next hire(s), revisit these goals and milestones to identify areas where you do not have either bandwidth or expertise. These are the areas to consider for new hires.

Second, review your current workload for you and the team. You and your initial team are *extremely* valuable. Given that your compensation is likely in the form of equity, your time is worth more than cash. With that in mind, your time should be spent driving the business forward, learning more about your customers, and working on needle-moving activities. When you find that you or someone on your team are working on repetitive or less valuable tasks, you can choose to hire in this area.

Hiring versus Outsourcing

Not all of those areas require a full-time hire. Much like the considerations for hiring engineering talent in Tactic 10, you should evaluate whether a long-term full-time hire is needed. For example, many startups choose to engage contract UX designers or fractional CFOs. These roles will most certainly be needed in the long term, but may not need a full-time resource in the short term.

When to Hire Generalists and Specialists

As your venture grows and matures, you will likely have far too many gaps in expertise to fill than you can afford to fill. For this reason, the professional profile of early team members differs from those you hire 12–24 months into the venture.

For example, you likely won't need a full-time employee specializing in media buying within the first six months. You will, however, need someone who can conduct the activities of a media buyer if you need to run an advertising campaign related to your goals. Your first marketing hire may be a marketing generalist who can help with advertising strategy, design, targeting, budgeting, and media buying.

Each generalist, however, must have a specialty. This specialty is their expertise. They are nimble and can work across functions—much like you now can after having explored each of the tactics—but they will provide long-term value to the venture through their expertise and leadership.

I am a great example of this. In the ventures I have built, I have served as a generalist across technology, marketing, operations, and more, tackling anything from advertising campaigns and content creation, and sales process, to infrastructure, DevOps, and even corporate IT! But my expertise had historically been in engineering. As time passes, you will hire specialists in all the areas previously addressed by generalists.

Writing the Job Description

Once you know who you need to hire it's time to craft the job description. Drafting a job description is not to be taken lightly—it presents your company to people who may potentially join the team. But attracting candidates is not the only purpose for drafting a job description.

Drafting a job description first and foremost helps you internally. For you personally, drafting the job description helps you develop an understanding of the role you're hiring for and what you are looking for in candidates. As you revise the description, you should socialize it with the rest of your team because this will help build alignment among everyone regarding the role you're hiring for. This enables everyone to get comfortable with the idea of a new team member joining and determine how each individual on the team can help prepare and set up the new hire for success. It also offers the rest of the team a chance to voice their own opinions on what's needed for the role in question.

Job descriptions also have external benefits beyond directly attracting talent. First, the job description will help friends of the venture—including investors, advisors, partners, and others who want the venture to succeed—understand the role. They can then narrow down their network to identify individuals who would be a good fit. Next, it helps friends of the venture to market the role far and wide.

Lastly, the written job description helps candidates understand your company, the role, and whether they are qualified. This applies both in the recruiting process and post-hire. During the recruiting process, it allows you and the candidate to determine fit. After you hire a candidate, they can refer back to the job description to ensure that they are meeting expectations.

So, what exactly should go in the job description? It should contain the following elements:

- Company Overview: Share a high-level description of the venture, including your long-term vision for impact. Also include any traction you have, as it helps de-risk the venture for potential candidates.
- Role Overview: Describe the role you are hiring for, how the individual will help advance the business, and how it fits into the existing team.
- Responsibilities: Create a bulleted list of the variety of responsibilities of the job.
- Requirements: Include all qualifications for applicants, including specific work experiences, technical skills, and education that you're looking for.
- Location and Travel: Include any location or geographic requirements as well as the percentage of time the individual must spend traveling.
- Compensation: In some regions, countries, and US states, you may be required to include compensation information in the job description. Consult local regulations before publishing.
- Call to Action: Be sure to include the next steps for interested applicants to get in touch. This might be an email address or an online application.

Rather than start from scratch, I highly recommend finding inspiration in job descriptions for similar roles at other startup ventures.

The candidates you speak with likely have plenty of opportunities in front of them, so you need to determine what sets you apart. With so many opportunities, candidates are looking for situations most likely to lead to their long-term success. How much you have achieved in the little time you have already spent building your venture will be a clear indicator. The traction from market testing and product development helps communicate the venture's potential and shouldn't be overlooked in the job description or during the recruiting process.

Since you are on the hunt for top-tier talent, I always recommend adding a note at the bottom for applicants who might not be a fit for the specific role to reach out to learn more. It's always possible they might be a fit for the team even if not for the specific role you're advertising.

Sourcing Candidates

Much like with sales in Tactic 6, you must fill your funnel of potential candidates for these open roles. You can take two approaches: reactive and proactive. Reactive allows you to take inbound inquiries from people interested in the role, whether they found it posted on a job board or had it forwarded to them by someone in their network. Proactive outreach is when you conduct research, find clearly qualified individuals, and make the first move.

Starting with reactive, identify watering holes where your ideal candidates likely exist. For example, if you are hiring engineers, you are highly likely to find them on StackOverflow, an online community for engineers. More generally, you will find job seekers interested in roles at startups through AngelList Talent (now Wellfound). You can also look to more traditional job posting websites. Once you have posted the job description online in these watering holes, you can review incoming resumes.

Remember that sometimes the best fit candidates will be people you already know! Be sure to share the job posting on your personal and company social media profiles. You can also ask friends of the company to share or repost the job descriptions to extend your reach.

A more proactive approach involves researching who might be a good fit for your role using a variety of online platforms. For example, in a situation where I was hiring a software engineer, I began my proactive research on LinkedIn. The first step was identifying individuals who met the qualifications. I was looking for a software engineer located in the Boston area with a passion for sustainability. I started with a simple LinkedIn search for "software engineer sustainability" located in Greater Boston at companies with fewer than 200 employees:

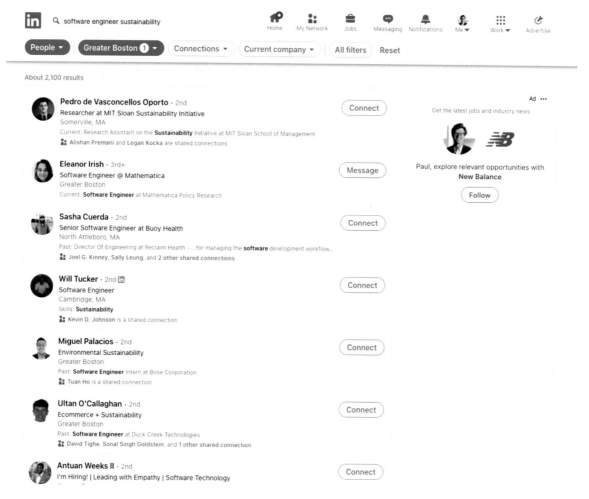

A LinkedIn search for new potential candidates using the search term "software engineer sustainability" with a filter for individuals located in Greater Boston yields 2,100 possible results.

This initial search yielded 2,100 results, although not all were strong fits based on their current work experience. After reviewing hundreds of profiles, I began narrowing down the results to those I believed could be a potential fit. I identified 15 individuals and sent connection requests to them with brief messages:

> *Hi [First Name], I noticed that you're also a software engineer interested in working on sustainability issues via technology. I am looking for someone who would be interested in joining us on our journey to keep plastic out of the ocean. We have a variety of technical needs and I'd love to connect. —Paul*

While not every outreach message yielded an accepted connection request or a response, a follow-up increased the number of responses:

> *Hey [First Name], Thanks for connecting. Are you open to having a chat about Oceanworks?*

In some sense, this is a numbers game, and more outreach yields more results. Remember, not everyone you reach out to will respond and those who do are not necessarily interested in a new role.

One thing you might consider is that most startups—yours included—provide stock options vesting over four years. Because startup employees don't want to miss out on those options if their current company is on track for an exit, it may make strategic sense to look for employees of startups who have been at the company for three or more years because they may be coming up on a full vesting. Similarly, many startups have a one-year cliff, meaning that employees receive about 25% of their stock after they hit the one-year mark of employment. Given that they have just received a lump sum of their stock options, you can consider individuals who have just passed a one-year anniversary mark at their startup. This does, however, introduce the risk that they could also stay with *your* venture for just one year, so be sure to understand why they are interested in new opportunities.

You can't interview everyone, so you need to whittle down the list before inviting everyone in for an interview. The first step is reviewing resumes to determine who might be a fit based on their prior experience. You should look at education and professional experience. Within their professional experience, you should look for relevant expertise, the ability to work cross-functionally as a generalist, and the outcomes they have produced. You should prioritize candidates into a must-interview category, backups, and those who are not a fit.

Interviewing

You also need to build a systematic review process to ensure you are bringing on the people who will help to move the venture forward.

For your interview process, prepare by determining who is on the search committee for the new hire and what you're looking for in interviews. A search committee sounds incredibly formal and—while you don't need a formal process—you do need a systematic process to avoid bad hires who can drain your time and energy. The committee should be composed of either your entire team or five people, whichever is smaller. It is also wise to introduce an individual who is not a member of your team into your hiring process, such as an advisor, investor, or other friend of the venture. They can provide an invaluable, outside perspective.

Next, align on what the search committee is looking for. This comes in the form of an interview guide. Your interview guide should include five to seven criteria of relevant experience or interpersonal characteristics you are evaluating candidates on. For example, when hiring a product manager, you might evaluate candidates based on criteria including product management skills/experience, product strategy, cross-functional team management, user research, intangibles, and fit with the current team.

Before having candidates meet with the entire committee, set up screener phone calls that last less than 30 minutes to determine whether they are an initial fit. For those who pass that screening, introduce them to two additional members of your search committee for further review based on the criteria in the interview guide. Each member of the search committee should provide an overall rating, such as must-hire, strong candidate, not best fit, or do not hire. These ratings should be the starting point for conversation among the search committee before making any hiring decisions.

In many cases you may choose to set up second- and even third-round interviews with those candidates who are highly qualified for the role. This can help to dig deeper about areas of interest or areas in which the candidate has potential weaknesses.

After the search committee settles on a candidate, take the time to conduct reference checks. For each individual to whom you're considering making a job offer, conduct at least two reference checks. You can ask the candidate for two references to speak with and you should also conduct any background research with any mutual connections you might have.

When possible, "try before you buy" by engaging a potential new hire in a longer interview in which they work with the team on addressing a business challenge or in a contract role for a period of weeks to months. With consideration for how to respect the candidate's time, the try-before-you-buy approach can be incredibly helpful for both parties. This will help both you and the potential new hire determine whether the fit is right.

Hire slow, fire fast. You can take your time bringing someone into the venture's team, but if they are not a fit, let them go quickly and move on.

Compensation Considerations

Hiring talent requires you to expend your other most precious resource: money. But the overall compensation for new hires does not need to be exclusively money, and in most cases, it shouldn't be. While cash is attractive, equity offers the opportunity to own a portion of the business, which can lead to far more upside than a cash salary provides. In most cases, you will want to offer a combination of stock options and cash compensation.

In the very early days, you can offer a variety of combinations of cash and stock to allow candidates to choose the compensation that best matches their current and long-term financial goals. For example, you might offer three options:

Option 1: $50,000 cash and 1% equity

Option 2: $75,000 cash and 0.5% equity

Option 3: $100,000 cash and 0.25% equity

For any stock offered as a part of a compensation package, make sure vesting is in place. Determine what works best for your situation, but the normal schedule is four years vesting with a one-year cliff and then 1/48 each month after that for the remaining three years.

Before you share any numbers with candidates, refer to compensation databases to understand what market rates look like at the given point in time.

Outside of cash and stock, consider the value of benefits including—but not limited to—health insurance.

Benefits

Beyond compensation, employees can be attracted to your company with benefits and perks. Some of these benefits are simple and straightforward, such as health insurance. Providing health insurance to employees is table stakes. It can be complex to set up, but many of the payroll and HR platforms have added features such as health insurance packages that make it quick and easy to begin offering this to your team. Similar to health insurance, most potential recruits may wish to see your retirement offerings, such as 401(k) packages. You might choose not to offer any matching for retirement contributions in the early days, but 401(k) availability is also table stakes. To avoid the administration overhead, you might also look to your HR platform for these benefits.

In addition to some benefits that are common across the board, you might choose to also offer other perks such as unlimited or generous vacation/paid time off, remote work flexibility, professional development budgets, wellness reimbursements, and free snacks in the office.

These additional perks can make a big difference in attracting talent as you grow but shouldn't be the sole reason extremely early employees join—you need them bought into the mission.

Setting New Hires up for Success

Aligning on a new role to hire for, identifying candidates, interviewing them, and narrowing down to your top choice is a lot of work. To ensure you're setting new hires up for success on day one, prepare onboarding and role-specific goals.

Onboarding, whether formal or informal, should introduce the new hire to the history of the company, the venture's purpose, and the people with whom they will build the future. You may also choose to introduce them to investors or advisors to provide visibility and create opportunities for the new hire to receive guidance and advice.

The first 90-day plan for each new hire should clarify how the individual's goals relate to the organizational-level goals from Tactic 1 and provide a list of actions you would recommend they take to be successful in their role. You can write down 20 recommendations, but to reinforce the entrepreneurial environment, let them know it is ultimately up to them what to prioritize and that these are simply recommendations.

Creating Culture

Expertise is not all you are looking for, however. Your venture has a culture that you and your co-founding team are building every minute of every day. You may not yet have this captured and articulated in a culture deck, but the values you possess, the actions you take, and the shared beliefs you hold define your culture. As a founder, you drive this culture forward. Each additional hire you make carries the culture on and changes it with their actions on a daily basis.

EXAMPLE

nurtur

Kristen Ellefson and Bindu Chanagala are the co-founders of nurtur, a digital health application that harnesses the power of AI to proactively enroll high-risk women in care plans proven to prevent postpartum depression. By teaming up with ob-gyns, nurtur improves outcomes for women and closes gaps in maternal mental health care through evidence-based self-guided therapy.

Knowing they needed to expand their team, Ellefson and Chanagala identified skills gaps, crafted a job description, wrote an outreach email to receive referrals, and also proactively filtered LinkedIn for relevant candidates and were able to find someone who was already a first-degree connection from a previous role, in addition to several highly qualified second-degree connections. Since these were warm introductions, they received a 100% response rate when Ellefson sent out messages.

Needing to narrow the search down to a highly qualified candidate, they also prepared an interview guide and potential compensation packages for the new recruit. Nurtur's structured and systematic approach increased the odds of bringing on the best-qualified candidate.

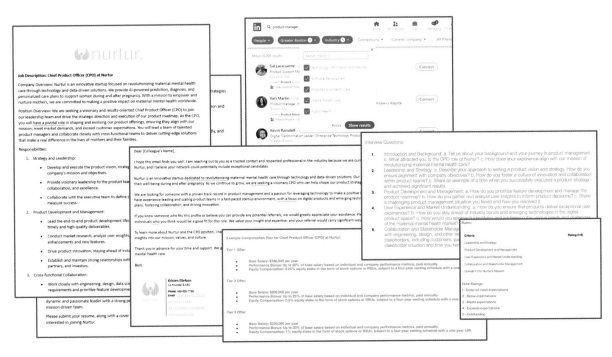

The nurtur team created a variety of assets for recruiting, including a job description, outreach emails, and potential compensation packages, and then sourced qualified candidates from LinkedIn.

Summary

Your job as the entrepreneurial leader is to build an amazing team. You have achieved traction that has unlocked fundraising and enabled you to bring more people on your team. You shouldn't hire until you need to and you shouldn't hire anyone who you don't have 100% confidence in because each new early hire has a dramatic impact on the culture of your team. You can find the right candidates by carefully crafting a job description, running your search with both proactive research and reactive resume review, and conducting rigorous interviews. Then it becomes your job to set your new hires up for success and you lead them and the rest of your team to create your future vision for the world. Hire slow, fire fast.

TOOLS OF THE TRADE

Job Posting

Wellfound (wellfound.com)

VentureFizz (venturefizz.com/jobs)

BuiltIn Jobs (builtin.com/jobs)

SnapHunt (snaphunt.com)

VentureLoop (ventureloop.com/ventureloop/home.php)

CrunchBoard (crunchboard.com)

Mashable Jobs (jobs.mashable.com/jobs/search/results)

Startup.jobs (startup.jobs)

Startuppers (startupers.com)

WeWorkRemotely (weworkremotely.com)

LinkedIn (linkedin.com)

ZipRecruiter (ziprecruiter.com)

Indeed (indeed.com)

Monster (monster.com)

Compensation

Carta Benchmarking (carta.com/benchmarking)

Pave (pave.com/benchmarking)

Wellfound (wellfound.com/hiring-data)

HR, Payroll, and Benefits

Gusto (gusto.com)

Deel (deel.com)

TriNet (trinet.com)

Paychex (paychex.com)

PROMPTS

1. Outline the values that matter to you.
2. Align on what values are necessary to succeed in your mission.
3. Draft version 1 of your culture code. Reflect on how well you live it every day.
4. Identify your next 10 hires and prioritize to fill your HR gaps.
5. Determine whether these 10 individuals are contractors or full-time hires.
6. Write a job description for the first hire (template available!).
7. Source candidates for the first role you're hiring for and build a pipeline.
8. Craft an outreach email to each identified candidate.
9. Determine the compensation structure for your first hire.

WORKBOOK

Get the Startup Tactics Pitch Deck Workbook, which will help identify skills gaps on your team, craft a job description, identify candidates, prepare to interview highly qualified candidates, and determine compensation. Within you will find worksheets that include:

1. Role Identification: You must first identify the most immediate need on the team.
2. Job Description: Define the role and responsibilities in a formal document.

3. Referral Outreach: Craft a recruiting email and send it to relevant individuals in your network.

4. Advertising: Share the job description far and wide to generate candidate interest.

5. Proactive Sourcing: Take a proactive targeted approach to recruit top-tier talent.

6. Interviewing: Determine the best structure to help you evaluate candidates.

7. Compensation: Determine what appropriate compensation should look like.

ADDITIONAL RESOURCES

→ **Get the Workbook!** Visit StartupTactics.net/hiring

NEXT STEPS

IF YOU'VE MADE IT this far, you and your venture have already been on quite a journey, whether it was founding a brand-new startup, creating a new product, or entering a new market. Let's take a moment to recap how we got here.

We began our exploration of the Startup Tactics methodology with foundations, including goal setting and systems. These goals help the venture stay focused on what truly must get done, skipping or postponing activities that don't help the business make progress toward reaching those goals. The systems enable us to track key metrics to measure our progress.

With the foundations in place, we moved forward to market testing. This begins with collecting additional market research. Based on those findings, we looked at how best to communicate the product's value proposition in a visual medium with assets, which provide the collateral for marketing and sales. To validate the efficacy of those assets and the resonance of our key messages, we use targeted digital advertising and outbound sales campaigns. These activities lead not just to confirmation that demand exists, but clarity regarding who the demand is from, which can inform what product should be built and any key requirements.

We then bring that product to life using product development tactics. Before actually building anything, we created a product roadmap to chart the course for the product over time, allowing us to set the plan for what to build and when to build it. We then tapped the design process to determine what the product should look like and how it will work. Those early designs were then tested using the user testing tactic. Only after several iterations was the design refined enough to begin full-scale engineering.

With an initial customer pool from market testing and a solution built from product development, it's time to acquire additional resources to advance the venture's development. Within the resource acquisition stage, we looked at how to incorporate the venture, along with other legal considerations, before exploring startup finance and the development of the financial model. Based on the financial model we designed a pitch deck that tells a story beyond just the facts and figures that engages the audience with a compelling narrative. Armed with a financial plan and pitch deck, we then mapped out how to execute a successful fundraising process. Finally, with the additional money secured through fundraising, we evaluated which roles to fill and how to find and attract the talent to fill them in the hiring tactic.

Now it's time to use the final workbook, the Skills Scorecard, to assess what you've learned throughout the book so you can better understand your current situation. Then you'll explore how everything fits together, how to stay scrappy, the importance of continuing to learn as you go, and how to change course when necessary. You'll also examine some leadership concerns, such as when to change hats and how to find the right work-life balance. You'll even discover a bonus tactic. All of this will help you on your entrepreneurial journey forward.

Workbook: Personal Skills Scorecard Post-Assessment

Now that you've learned the tactics, use the Skills Scorecard Workbook to rate your experience and comfort level with each of the tactical skills that an entrepreneur needs. You can use this to compare your preassessment to your post-assessment and see where you might need to revisit some tactics to further strengthen your skills.

ADDITIONAL RESOURCES

→ **Download the Post-Assessment and Reflection!** Visit StartupTactics.net/scorecard

---

Putting Together the Puzzle

I'm so excited that you've read this book and that another venture can benefit from these tactics. While you now have a structured approach to turning your business plan into a business, don't forget the basic axiom captured so simply in an Albert Einstein quote: "The only source of knowledge is experience." You now have the methodology and tactics, but to gain true knowledge you must apply them in real life. These tactics are applicable in a variety of settings. You've made your way through the tactics needed whether you're founding a new startup, joining an existing startup, or launching a new initiative within an established organization. These tactics provide you with the day 0 mindset and skills to build new things that move the needle.

Many organizations—especially publicly traded companies—view this solely in terms of driving revenue growth or profit margins. Don't be fooled. Moving the needle as an entrepreneur should be about the amount of positive impact you can have in the world.

As you explore the tactics and how they apply in the real world, you will find that they form a puzzle of sorts. Each tactic represents a piece of the puzzle and each connects in ways that may not be obvious at first. While some of the connections between tactics are clearly called out in this book, you will discover others as you go. Understanding how they relate to each other will make you a stronger, more efficient entrepreneur.

If you are a hardcore puzzler, you might consider referring to the picture on the box as "cheating." But in this case, the picture on the box is your business plan and it's imperative to refer back to it frequently to determine how the pieces come together. It will also increase the odds of these tactics leading to successful experiments.

Staying Scrappy: Order of Operations

The spirit of Startup Tactics is to learn and initially execute them in a specific order. But after the first go-round, they can be used iteratively throughout the life cycle of your entire venture. You should initially follow the tactics in sequence but recognize that once you apply a tactic you're not done with it and may need to revisit it often.

When you're set with the foundations and begin testing the market, those foundations don't remain set in stone. You should continually revisit and revise your goals and systems. As you transition from market testing to product development, you need to continue testing the market to optimize your business and ensure your product continues meeting customer needs, which may change significantly.

Foundations, market testing, and product development certainly don't stop when you begin fundraising and hiring. In fact, the velocity you have with these earlier tactics helps you demonstrate the effectiveness of you and your team during the fundraising and hiring processes.

Waiting to build the product until after testing the market, for example, makes you scrappy. By patiently waiting to build the right product instead of jumping directly into something that isn't yet market tested further conserves your resources.

When applying any of the tactics, remember that you can waste a lot of time applying them if they aren't aligned with the goals determined in the first tactic. Neglecting to continually ensure alignment between your actions and goals inevitably leads to squandered resources and opportunities.

Iterating on Your Experiments

Entrepreneurship tactics, or actions, are not one-and-done. Apply the tactics in a way that helps you learn because those learnings will allow you to optimize your business and provide the best possible chances of long-term impact.

Hopefully, you still have your lab coat on. Scientists continue tweaking their experiments until they find something that works and even then keep making adjustments as they further refine and iterate. There's always another experiment ready to be run and unlock additional insights.

Course Correction

If you have followed the tactics through each of the four stages with an iterative approach you've likely transitioned from the jungle, where there is little direction and line of sight is limited, to the dirt road where there is a clear path but still much to figure out, to the highway where the business can scale. This concept of transitioning from the jungle to the highway was introduced by Jeff Bussgang in his 2017 book, *Entering StartUpLand*. Now you should be in a place where you can lift off towards your venture's North Star.

Keep in mind that if you can't move forward with the venture because customers don't want what you think they do or your team isn't right, you should revise. If this venture doesn't have legs, pivot. But if things truly aren't panning out, ignore the term "never give up" and instead consider whether a rapid unscheduled disassembly, a phrase used in the aerospace industry to describe an unintentional catastrophic failure of a rocket or other spacecraft, is the best path forward. While you might not have intended for the business to fail, it's okay, and it is better to make a determination quickly rather than drag it out over months or even years.

Don't keep pushing if there isn't a path to greatness. Instead, consider whether there is another path to your personal North Star—whether that is with the same team, the same idea, or neither.

Leading Your Team: OTC

In the US Navy the OTC, or Officer in Tactical Command, is an officer in tactical command of a group of ships. This leader provides direction, guiding the group to achieve the desired end result. As your team's leader, you're providing direction for each of your ships, or co-founders, with regard to which tactics get employed and when.

In your role, however, you are responsible not just for the tactics but also for the strategy and planning. Tactics when executed alone, in isolation, and without regard for the strategy and plan leads to completely wasted resources, of which you have a very limited supply aboard your ships. But when you are the senior officer in possession of unique knowledge and perspective, it is critical that you train and show your team what actions to take and which tactics to apply.

Changing Hats

Each tactic we've covered represents training for a role that you'll need to fill or a hat that you'll get to wear. As a startup founder, you'll likely put these hats on in rapid succession and then wear them all simultaneously. If you join an existing startup, you'll probably need to wear some combination of hats at different points in time depending on the startup's stage and staffing. But remember, it's equally important to know when to put hats on and when to take them off. We can't do everything forever, and your ability to delegate is integral to your organization's success.

In a larger organization, you may find there is a time and place to swap out your hats. There you might leverage the tactics to become the most amazing product manager Amazon has ever seen. Or you might be leading a new internal venture and face the double-edged sword of having a variety of resources but not ones that fit the small nimble team you must build.

I recall the work I did within a large public company that was building a new product as part of an innovation team. Housed in the dimly lit basement of a large office building, we were a small but mighty team. Conventional wisdom might indicate that my *move-fast-and-break-things* mentality would cause problems within such a large organization. But I found what held me back most was failing to determine when to put hats on and take them off. There was an alliance I built during my time there that moved the needle. Eventually, I realized I had to take the partnership development hat off to get back to my primary focus.

Successful CEOs can't spend all their time writing code or wading deep into the detailed analytics of a specific marketing campaign. Knowing when to pass the torch to a specialist is just as important as identifying which ones to hire and when.

In Tactic 15, Hiring, we looked at how each member of the early team should be a generalist with a specialty. That includes you. However, your long-term job is leading the team to achieve the mission. If your specialty today is engineering or marketing, you must learn to hand those responsibilities off to highly qualified team members you bring on board in the medium and long term. As the leader of the organization, you must devote your time to strategy. Tactics will help you get to that point, and help you guide your team as they execute those tactics in the future.

Finding Balance While Building a Business

As a founder, you're responsible for everything until you have enough traction to unlock more resources. Then you can begin bringing on others who can help you take off some of those hats you've been wearing. Of course, if you've reached this point you've had a lot on your plate and it's easy to get overwhelmed. It may be hard to let go and trust that others can manage this or that part of your "baby."

But constant evaluation of your workload and work-life balance is necessary to protect yourself from negative mental health effects. There is a careful balance between being a scrappy entrepreneur and being so scrappy that the unhealthy workload negatively impacts your happiness.

Your happiness may also flag at times in the face of failure. But startups are all about experimentation, and lots of times those fail but still teach us something. You might also fail at times yourself, which is more likely when you're spread thin and the less focused you are on your primary tasks and objectives. Everything matters, but a diminished happiness and spirit can impede your continued ability to work towards your vision.

My colleague and an Entrepreneur in Residence at the Trust Center, Susan Neal, began teaching a course in happiness. She reminds students that "It's okay to be down and to feel this emotion and feel miserable that it didn't work out or something you really hoped for didn't happen." She prompts students to "Be realistic; experience those down moments, because that's life. By experiencing those moments, you'll then be able to really enjoy it when things are good or you do get what you want."

Don't do so much that your mental or physical health suffers—find the balance that works best for you.

Bonus Tactic: The Update Email

While you, as an entrepreneurial leader, will have the help of your team, you should also leverage the help of your network. As you apply the tactics to your business plan and make some initial progress, don't miss the opportunity to solicit the help of others. Entrepreneurship is a difficult endeavor and many people will be rooting for your success. Build your support system to include advisors, investors, and others supporting your progress.

As you move forward on your entrepreneurial journey, you must be held accountable, and holding yourself accountable doesn't cut it. But this ecosystem of stakeholders and supporters does. However, you will need to be a little proactive.

The update email shares your progress and gives you a platform to ask for help. You will be expected to send the update email to investors, for example, but you should share it with others as well. Consider this a bonus tactic!

Your update email should be sent on a regular cadence, most likely monthly. It should provide an update to your venture's closest circle, share progress against goals, and solicit the help you need most. This means including metrics even when they aren't as strong as you'd like. Transparency breeds trust and helps you remain accountable to your goals.

Encourage your network to forward the update email and suggest others who should receive the email on a regular basis. It is a great tool for growing your support network!

Everyone has a different format and length they prefer, but be sure to include some of these components:

1. TLDR: Many people receive a lot of these updates, so always include a summary at the top.
2. Metrics: Include your venture's most important metrics on a consistent basis. Be sure to include absolute numbers as well as an indication of how these metrics have changed since the last update. If you drop a KPI for something new, explain the rationale behind that move.
3. Strategy: Sharing an update on your learnings, experiments, and venture strategy will keep your audience informed and excited about where you're going!
4. Product Updates: Show and tell what changed with the product.
5. Financials: In some cases, specifically with investors, you may choose to include your company's financials in the update email.
6. Customers: Show photos or quotes from real customers whenever possible!
7. Asks: The most important part is asking for help in specific areas. This might be introductions to customers, new hires, press coverage, feedback, and so on. If the ask is too vague, no one will know what it is you really want, so make it something concrete.

The time to start sending your update is *right now*. Don't wait to share your progress and build out your support network. If you're unsure of who to include, start with me! Add paulcheek@ paulcheek.com to your update emails!

We Need More Entrepreneurs

Don't keep these tactics to yourself. With all of the problems that we are creating for ourselves as a society, we need more entrepreneurs. You are now well equipped with the tactics in this book and I encourage you to help others become more entrepreneurial. More people we have who are thinking and acting entrepreneurially is a good thing.

With your newfound knowledge I ask you to please share what you have learned with others. As you apply the tactics in this book, please document the experiments you run, including both success and failure, to show others how they too can take action as entrepreneurs. Your work will serve as an inspiration to the next generation of innovation-driven entrepreneurs.

Don't just document your work; if you wish for it to have an impact you need to share it. You should share it in whatever form you are comfortable with and if you are open to sharing more broadly, please post it to our website to be showcased to others who are employing tactics to build new ventures and new products!

ADDITIONAL RESOURCES

→ **Share Your Work!** Visit StartupTactics.net/share to submit examples of how you have employed the Tactics. You're sure to inspire others!

EDUCATOR MATERIALS

MANY ADDITIONAL RESOURCES ARE available online for you to leverage if you're a teacher, instructor, advisor, corporate innovation facilitator, or support startups in any way. If you are an educator, you can access everything you need to teach Startup Tactics in a full-semester course, ad hoc workshops, office hours, or in providing general feedback, including:

- Syllabus: Get a copy of the syllabus for the course that we teach at MIT, Venture Creation Tactics.
- Quizzes: Ensure your students are following along and understand the tactics in the context of building a new venture with 15 mini quizzes.
- Recorded Videos: Access short-form videos that explore each tactic with real-world examples.
- Slides: Leverage the slides used in the Tactics class at MIT to get started in customizing the content and cases for your students.
- Workshop Prompts: Prepare your students for success by hosting workshops for each tactic using the predefined prompts that help them get moving.
- Workbooks: Get 15 workbooks with 75-plus worksheets for students to build a foundation to execute each of the tactics for their venture.
- Playbook Assignments: Download sample assignments that provide the structure necessary for entrepreneurs to learn the tactics.

As an educator you can leverage these resources to seamlessly teach more and more entrepreneurs by following this flow:

- Assign the **book reading** in advance of a class or workshop.
- Optionally, assign the **quiz** to get students thinking.
- Share the **recorded videos** for students to access asynchronously.

- Use the **slides** to provide framing at the start of the class or workshop.
- Share the **workshop prompts** for students to work on during the class or workshop.
- Provide the tactic **workbooks** for students to explore each aspect of the tactic at their own pace and reflect on their learnings.
- Assign the **playbook assignment** as homework for completion.

If there are other resources that you would find helpful, just let us know and we would be glad to share what we have to make sure that you are best prepared to educate more entrepreneurs!

ADDITIONAL RESOURCES

→ **Get the Educator Materials!** Visit StartupTactics.net/educators where you can download slides, assignments, and more!

INDEX